SECOND STEPS IN READING AND WRITING

Second Edition

JACK WIGFIELD

Director: Laurie E. Likoff
Production Coordinator: Cynthia Funkhouser
Production: Carlisle Publishers Services
Printer and Binder: Malloy Lithographing

Newbury House
A division of HarperCollins Publishers

Language Science
Language Teaching
Language Learning

Second Steps in Reading and Writing, Second Edition

ISBN: 0-06-500053-6

94 93 92 91 9 8 7 5 4 3 2 1

Dedication

To
the Students, Faculty, Administration, and Staff,
Past and Present, of
Alemany Community College Center,
San Francisco

Contents

Preface

I am a practitioner in the field of ESL adult literacy. This book was written for other practitioners, those who meet a class daily, those who have to *do* something with that group, those who would like to develop their own materials just for their class, certainly the most sensible thing to do, but who, for a number of reasons, can't.

Second Steps in Reading and Writing is the second volume of a revision of *The Gateway to English Series: Book 1.* It continues these practices from the original book:

1. Self-contained lessons
2. The same format with the same type of tasks for each lesson
3. At least one task in each lesson for each developmental level in a class of mixed levels.

This volume contains these new features as well:

1. It presupposes the achievement of the objectives of Volume 1 of the revision and, therefore, narrows the developmental levels within a class, in that there is very little time given to letter formation.
2. It places more emphasis on the practical uses of literacy, in that most lessons end with a task which calls for a more complicated manipulation of literacy skills.
3. It calls for overt behavioral responses to some reading material, in that students follow written directions to complete a picture.
4. It provides two kinds of dictation: A *single word type* based on a regular sound/spelling pattern as well as *a simple sentence type* that calls for punctuation.

I owe a great deal to many of the people I teach with at Alemany and in the San Francisco Community College District, as well as to practice teachers, to visitors to my classes, and to people I've corresponded with. I also want to acknowledge my students who, by their mistakes and successes, have shown me what direction to take.

I would especially like to acknowledge the help of Nicolar Chang, my Director, and especially Peggy Doherty, Assistant Director, for the support that they have given me in continuing my classes.

I also appreciate the help I received from Laurie E. Likoff and Cindy Funkhouser of Newbury House and Diane Beausoleil of Carlisle Publishers Services.

Introduction to the Teacher

This is the second of a two volume revision of *First Steps in Reading and Writing*. The following goals of the first volume are the literacy prerequisites for this book: Students should be able to do the following:

1. Write the 26 letters of the English alphabet in a script of their choice.
2. Write some words.
3. Read those words.
4. Read and write some requested information on a standard form.
5. Write a list of dictated, regularly spelled, common English words.

While studying from the first volume, students should also have been developing their oral fluency, which by now should be more than that of a beginning student. The higher the oral fluency level, the better for using this volume.

The goals of this book are as follows:

Students will be able to do the following:

1. Write a 20–40 word note that matches their oral development. That is, if a student can say to his landlord, "Hey, Jim, my sink no good," his note might read:

8–15–90

DEAR JIM,
    MY SINK NO GOOD.
    LEE—APT. 201

2. Read and follow a list of instructions.
3. Read a simple narrative passage independently.
4. Recode in order to decode a word in their oral vocabulary. That is, guess at the pronunciation of a new word in order to understand it.
5. Write a short dictated message.
6. Read a calendar.
7. Look up a word in a dictionary.
8. Fill out most items on a standard form.

Like the first volume, this is a workbook. Students are given tasks that remain the same type throughout the book. The tasks vary in difficulty **within** a lesson. They are not all easy in Lesson 1 and all difficult in Lesson 40. There is a wide spectrum of literacy and oral fluency development in most literacy classes. Each lesson must contain material within each student's range. In each lesson, students should feel free to complete the tasks they can and ignore those that are too difficult or too easy. Evaluate your student's performance by comparing the tasks they do and those they ignore in Lesson 1 with the tasks they do and those they ignore in Lesson 40.

These are the principal tasks in each lesson:

1. **FILL OUT:** Students fill out samples from a standard form.
2. **READ ALOUD:** Students practice a simple dialogue that presents the main idea of the whole lesson. One person in the dialogue is given an extremely easy reading task that allows even the beginner to participate. The dialogue follows infor-

mal spoken English as closely as possible. This is the easiest reading material in each lesson and is usually associated with an accompanying picture.

3. **DIRECTIONS:** Students read instructions related to the lesson's picture and then perform the action. They either color, draw, or write on the picture.

4. **READ:** Students read this typical, titled, upper/lowercase, paragraphed reading task to themselves or preferably to the teacher and class.

5. **UP/DOWN:** Students find and write down contrasts or opposites from within the lesson to broaden their vocabulary.

6. **READ AND WRITE:** Students write one word in a blank in a paragraph dealing with the topic of the lesson. Students who successfully perform this task show that they can read independently.

7. **LISTEN AND WRITE:** Students write from dictation, one technique now used by the Immigration and Naturalization Service to test literacy development. They write full sentences from one to several words in a dialogue context:

      1: LET'S GO.

      2: WHY?

      1: IT'S LATE.

      2: I SEE. OK.

and four words in a list that follow a regular sound/symbol correspondence:

      A. FINE

      B. MINE

      C. NINE

      D. WINE

8. **WRITE A NOTE:** Students write a note and letter using the accepted form with a date, salutation, paragraphed body, and signature. Like the note in the first volume, this task uses the *Language Experience Approach,* which draws subject matter, grammar, and meaning from the student. Studies have shown that notes and letters are one of the most common uses of literacy.

9. **COPY:** Students copy two types of script in the first few lessons to review what was presented in Volume 1.

10. **DIRECTIONS:** Students carry out the instructions presented. The activities are usually based on the content of the lesson, but are not related to the picture as in the first DIRECTIONS.

11. **APPOINTMENT CALENDAR** (in the appendix): Students make a calendar for each month of the semester. It is treated as an appointment calendar and a journal. At the beginning of each month, they write down coming events, like holidays for the month. Every day they write one personal sentence in the square for that day. The sentence can range from "ME," to "TODAY IS MONDAY," to "I GOT A NEW JOB YESTERDAY."

12. **MY DICTIONARY** (in the appendix): Students write new words that usually arise in the WRITE A NOTE section. The words can be those they use orally but they can't spell yet, or words whose meanings they have not learned. They can either use a translation from their language (e.g. HOUSE = CASA), or draw a picture of the meaning (e.g., HOUSE = 🏠). The teacher helps only once. When they have trouble later, they should look up the word on their own.

13. **FIELD TRIPS—VIDEOTAPES:** Field trips and videotapes are not tasks, but are very important in literacy classes. Students visit and observe places pertinent to the topic of the lesson. For example, visit a local courtroom or view a videotape of courtroom scenes from NBC's *"LA Law"* in Lesson 17, In Court.

The Teacher's Manual for this book gives detailed suggestions for each lesson. A typical lesson might proceed like this:

1. Start the class by using the appointment calendar. Have each student write one short sentence for the day. Go around to help and respond to each student's sentence.

2. Present the dialogue. Write it on the board or on an overhead transparency to ensure that students look where you want them to. Ask the students to talk about the picture and its meaning first. Introduce realia. Talk about the topic. Relate the dialogue to the picture and, always looking at the dialogue, practice it to the point of memorization. Finish by using the technique explained in volume 1 for sound/symbol correspondences in the dialogue.

3. Let the class work individually, in pairs, in groups, or however they choose to complete the rest of the tasks.

   a. Place a box of colored crayons or color pencils in the front of the room to encourage movement and group help.

   b. Move around the room and work with individuals.

   c. Carry a small piece of scrap paper to write down new words for students who ask for help. Help them put their new word in their dictionary in the appendix.

   d. Take individuals or small groups with a common problem to the board and work on sound/symbol correspondences.

   e. Ask individuals to read READ, WRITE A NOTE, READ ALOUD to you. Choose the task that matches their development level.

   f. Help, but try not to give answers to UP/DOWN or READ AND WRITE. Encourage group work.

4. Bring the class together and give the dictation, LISTEN AND WRITE.

5. Ask students to write the answers to UP/DOWN or READ AND WRITE on the board.

6. If there is time left, have volunteers read aloud their notes or anything else in the lesson.

For the first one or even two weeks, it is important that all the tasks be done as a group. Many, if not all the tasks will be new, and students should be shown clearly what is expected of them.

In WRITE A NOTE, the whole class can compose one common note at first. After two weeks, however, students should be put on their own.

LESSON 1 Hello

FILL OUT

NAME _____

         (FIRST NAME)   (MIDDLE NAME)   (FAMILY NAME)

ADDRESS _____

         (NUMBER)   (STREET)   APT. #

_____

         (CITY)   (STATE)   (ZIP CODE)

TELEPHONE (_____) _____ – _____   U.S. CITIZEN — YES ☐ NO ☐

    (AREA CODE)

BIRTHDATE _____   SEX — MALE ☐ FEMALE ☐

    (MONTH/DAY/YEAR)

BIRTHPLACE _____ NATIVE LANGUAGE _____

SOCIAL SECURITY NUMBER _____ – _____ – _____

COLOR OF HAIR _____ COLOR OF EYES _____ HEIGHT _____ WEIGHT _____

READ ALOUD

1: GOOD MORNING.   1: HI.

2: WHAT?   2: WHAT?

1: HELLO.   1: NEVER MIND.

2: WHAT?   2: OK.

DIRECTIONS: LOOK AT THE PICTURE. DRAW. COLOR.

1. THE WOMAN HAS A BROWN DRESS.
2. THE MAN HAS A BLACK SUIT.
3. DRAW A TREE. THE TREE IS GREEN.
4. DRAW A CAR. THE CAR IS RED.
5. DRAW THE SUN. THE SUN IS YELLOW.

READ

HELLO

I am in class. I am in my class. I am in my new class. I am in my new class now. Good afternoon, everybody. Hello, everybody. Hi, everybody.

UP/DOWN

1. UP __ __ __   2. YOUR __ __   3. YOU __   4. OLD __ __   5. OUT __ __

READ AND WRITE

MY NEW CLASS

HI. THIS IS MY CLASS. HELLO. THIS _____ MY NEW CLASS.

GOOD EVENING. THIS IS _____ NEW CLASS TODAY.

GOOD EVENING TO YOU. _____ EVENING TO YOU ALL.

DIRECTIONS:

WHO IS IN YOUR CLASS?

1. NAME _____	TELEPHONE _____
2. NAME _____	BIRTHDATE _____
3. NAME _____	ZIP CODE_____
4. NAME _____	HEIGHT _____
5. NAME _____	COLOR OF HAIR _____
6. NAME _____	BIRTHPLACE_____
7. NAME _____	STREET _____
8. NAME _____	WEIGHT _____
9. NAME _____	COLOR OF EYES _____
10. NAME _____	TEACHER'S NAME _____

COPY

↓| T→ L⌐ ⌐⋮

↓| || ↓ H H⋮

↓| L→ L⌐

↓| T→ T⋮

↓| F F→ F⋮

↓| F F→ E E⋮

HI

I

HELLO

LESSON 2 Goodbye

READ ALOUD

1: I'M GOING TO WORK.

2: OK.

1: GOODBYE.

2: GOODBYE.

1: SO LONG.

2: SO LONG.

1: SEE YOU.

2: SEE YOU.

1: BYE BYE.

2: OK, OK. GO.

DIRECTIONS: LOOK AT THE PICTURE. DRAW. COLOR.

1. THE WOMAN HAS A GREEN DRESS.

2. THE MAN HAS A BLUE JACKET.

3. DRAW A CLOCK ON THE WALL. IT IS 7:15.

4. DRAW A WINDOW.

5. DRAW THE SUN OUTSIDE THE WINDOW.

6. DRAW A PICTURE ON THE WALL.

READ

GOODBYE

Look at the picture. Look at the man. Look at the woman.

It is morning. It is 7:15 in the morning. The man is going. the man is going to work.

Is the woman going to work later? Maybe.

UP/DOWN

1. HELLO _ _ _ _ _ _   2. FIRST _ _ _ _   3. MAN _ _ _ _ _

READ AND WRITE

GOING?

ARE YOU GOING? SAY, "GOODBYE."

ARE _____ GOING? SAY, "SO LONG" TO YOUR WIFE.

_____ YOU GOING? SAY, "SEE YOU" TO YOUR HUSBAND.

ARE YOU GOING? SAY, "BYE _____" TO YOUR CHILDREN.

ARE YOU GOING? YES? NOW? YES? OK. _____ .

LISTEN AND WRITE

1: _____ A. _____

2: _____ B. _____

1: _____ C. _____

2: _____ D. _____

WRITE A NOTE

(DATE) _____

_____

_____

_____

_____

_____

_____

_____

(SIGNATURE) _____

COPY

C C

C G G G

C O O

C O Q Q

C S S

GO

SO

SEE

IS

IT

LESSON 3 Beautiful

READ ALOUD

1: LOOK AT THE PICTURE.

2: OK.

1: LOOK AT THE CLOUD.

2: BEAUTIFUL

1: LOOK AT THE TREES.

2: BEAUTIFUL.

1: LOOK AT THE GRASS.

2: BEAUTIFUL.

1: LOOK AT THE MAN.

2: UGLY.

1: OK, OK.

DIRECTIONS: LOOK AT THE PICTURE. COLOR. WRITE. DRAW.

1. THE MAN HAS A RED JACKET.

2. THE MAN HAS BLACK PANTS.

3. THE MAN HAS AN ORANGE BACKPACK.

4. DRAW THE SUN IN THE SKY. THE SUN IS YELLOW.

5. THE SKY IS BLUE.

6. THE TREES ARE RED AND YELLOW.

7. THE GRASS IS GREEN.

READ

OUTSIDE

Go outside. Go out of the city. Walk in the countryside. Look around you. Look at the grass. Look at the trees. Look at the sky. Look at the clouds. Look at the hills. Look at the mountains. Everything is beautiful.

UP/DOWN

1. WOMAN _ _ _   2. LAST _ _ _ _ _   3. UGLY _ _ _ _ _ _ _ _ _ _

READ AND WRITE

BEAUTIFUL

LOOK AT THE PICTURE. IT IS BEAUTIFUL. _____ AT THE SKY. IT IS BEAUTIFUL. LOOK _____ THE CLOUD. IT IS BEAUTIFUL. LOOK AT _____ TREES. THEY ARE BEAUTIFUL. LOOK AT THE _____ . IT IS BEAUTIFUL.

COME ON. LET'S GO. LET'S _____ OUTSIDE. LET'S GO OUT OF THE CITY.

I _____

_____

LISTEN AND WRITE

1: _____   A. _____
2: _____   B. _____
1: _____   C. _____
2: _____   D. _____

WRITE A NOTE

(DATE) _____

_____

    _____

_____

_____

_____

_____

(SIGNATURE) _____

COPY

↓I	I⬊	M⬋	M↓	M
↓I	N↓	N↓	N	
↓I	K⬋	K⬋	K	
↓I	W⬋	W⬋	W↓	W
⬋/	∧↑	A→	A	
⬋/	X⬋	X		
→7	7⬋	Z⬋	Z	

LOOK   GO

OUT   THE

LESSON 4   A Pay Phone

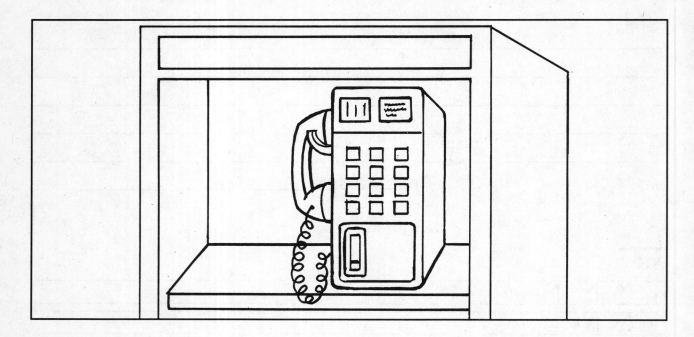

READ ALOUD

1: HEY, CALL HOME.
2: HOW?
1: PICK UP THE PHONE.
2: OK.
1: STOP.
2: OK.

1: LISTEN FOR THE TONE.
2: OK.
1: DEPOSIT MONEY.
2: OK.
1: DIAL.
2: OK. THANKS.
1: OK.

DIRECTIONS: LOOK AT THE PICTURE. DRAW. COLOR. WRITE.

1. THE PHONE BOOTH IS BLUE.
2. THE TELEPHONE IS BLACK.
3. DRAW A TELEPHONE BOOK. IT IS ON THE LEFT. THE PHONE BOOK IS RED.
4. LOOK AT THE DIAL. WRITE 1, 2, 3, 4, 5, 6, 7, 8, 9, 0.
5. WRITE **PHONE** ON THE BOOTH ABOVE THE PHONE.

READ

A PAY PHONE

Look at the picture. Look at the pay phone.

Call home. Call a friend. Call the doctor. How? Pick up the phone. Stop. Listen for the tone. Deposit money. Dial. Wait. Talk.

UP/DOWN

1. FIRST _ _ _ _   2. FREE _ _ _ _   3. TALK _ _ _ _ _ _ _

READ AND WRITE

PAY PHONES

PAY PHONES ARE EVERYWHERE. PAY PHONES ARE _____ GAS STATIONS. PAY PHONES ARE IN STORES. _____ PHONES ARE IN SCHOOLS. PAY PHONES _____ IN HOSPITALS. PAY PHONES ARE ON THE STREET.

_____ UP THE PHONE. STOP. LISTEN FOR THE _____ DEPOSIT MONEY. DIAL. WAIT. TALK. IT _____ EASY.

LISTEN AND WRITE

1: _____   A. _____
2: _____   B. _____
1: _____   C. _____
2: _____   D. _____

WRITE A NOTE

(DATE) _____

_____

_____

_____

_____

_____

_____

_____

(SIGNATURE) _____

COPY

↓| D↓ D

↓| P↓ P

↓| P↓ B↓ B

↓| P↓ R↓ R

PHONE

STOP

LISTEN

CALL

MONEY

DIAL

LESSON 5   Watching TV

READ ALOUD

1: LOOK AT THE PICTURE.

2: OK.

1: THEY ARE WATCHING CHANNEL 2.

2: WRONG.

1: THEY ARE WATCHNG CHANNEL 5.

2: WRONG.

1: THEY ARE WATCHING CHANNEL 9.

2: WRONG.

1: THEY ARE WATCHING CHANNEL 4.

2: RIGHT.

1: OK.

DIRECTIONS: LOOK AT THE PICTURE. DRAW. COLOR.

1. THE WOMAN HAS A RED BLOUSE.

2. THE MAN IN THE CHAIR HAS A GREEN SHIRT.

3. THE MAN ON TV HAS A BLUE SHIRT.

4. DRAW A WINDOW BEHIND THE PEOPLE.

5. DRAW THE MOON OUTSIDE THE WINDOW.

READ

TV

Do you watch TV? Do you like TV? What channel do you watch? Do you watch channel 2? Do you watch channel 5? Do you watch channel 7? Do you watch channel 9?

I don't like TV. I don't like to listen and watch. I like to talk.

UP/DOWN

1. MAN _ _ _ _ _ _   2. IN FRONT OF _ _ _ _ _ _   3. RIGHT _ _ _ _ _ _

READ AND WRITE

WATCH TV

I WATCH TV EVERY DAY. I WATCH _____ EVERY NIGHT. I LIKE TV.

SOMETIMES I _____ CHANNEL 2. SOMETIMES I WATCH CHANNEL 5. SOMETIMES _____ WATCH CHANNEL 7. SOMETIMES I WATCH CHANNEL _____ . SOMETIMES I WATCH CHANNEL 9.

CHANNEL _____ IS THE BEST.

I _____

_____

LISTEN AND WRITE

1: _____   A. _____

2: _____   B. _____

1: _____   C. _____

2: _____   D. _____

WRITE A NOTE

(DATE) _____

_____

_____

_____

_____

_____

_____

_____

(SIGNATURE) _____

COPY

J J J J

U U U

V V V

Y Y Y

WATCH

TV

CHANNEL

4   5   7   9   2   3

LESSON 6   Fish

FILL OUT

_____
(FAMILY NAME)   (FIRST NAME)   (MIDDLE NAME)

SOCIAL SECURITY NUMBER _____ – _____ – _____

READ ALOUD

1: I LIKE FISH.

2: OH?

1: I LIKE TO LOOK AT FISH.

2: OH?

1: I LIKE TO GO FISHING.

2: OH?

1: I LIKE TO EAT FISH.

2: OK, OK.

DIRECTIONS: LOOK AT THE PICTURE. DRAW. COLOR.

1. THE WATER IS BLUE.
2. DRAW THE SUN IN THE SKY. THE SUN IS YELLOW.
3. DRAW A BOAT IN THE WATER.
4. DRAW FISH IN THE WATER.
5. THE BOAT HOUSE IS BROWN.
6. WRITE **FISH** ON THE SIGN.
7. DRAW 2 CLOUDS IN THE SKY.

READ

FISH

Look at the picture. That is me. I am fishing. I like to go fishing. I like to look at fish in the water. Fish are beautiful.

I like to catch fish. I like to cook fish. I like to eat fish, too. Fish is good for you. Come on. Let's go fishing.

UP/DOWN

1. YOU __   2. YOU __ __   3. HATE __ __ __ __   4. UGLY __ __ __ __ __ __ __ __ __ __

READ AND WRITE

FISHING

MANY PEOPLE LIKE TO FISH. MEN LIKE _____ FISH. WOMEN LIKE TO FISH. BOYS LIKE TO _____ . GIRLS LIKE TO FISH.

PEOPLE FISH EVERYWHERE. _____ FISH IN LAKES. PEOPLE FISH IN RIVERS. PEOPLE _____ IN THE OCEAN.

COME ON. LET'S _____ FISHING.

I _____

_____

LISTEN AND WRITE

1: _____   A. _____

2: _____   B. _____

1: _____   C. _____

2: _____   D. _____

WRITE A NOTE

(DATE) _____

_____

_____

_____

_____

_____

_____

(SIGNATURE) _____

COPY

y x a

y x a, a a

y x a, a a

y x a, d d d

y x a, q g g

y x a, q g g g

Fish   fish

in

good   Go

the   The

Like   like

LESSON 7 Wake Up

READ ALOUD

1: HEY, WAKE UP.

2: MMMMMMMMM.

1: HEY, GET UP.

2: MMMMMMMMM.

1: IT'S LATE, BOB.

2: I'M NOT BOB.

1: OK, OK.

DIRECTIONS: LOOK AT THE PICTURE. DRAW. COLOR.

1. THE WOMAN HAS A RED DRESS.
2. THE LAMP IS YELLOW.
3. THE TOP SHEET IS BLUE.
4. THE BOTTOM SHEET IS GREEN.
5. THE PILLOW IS ORANGE.
6. DRAW A PICTURE ON THE WALL. DRAW YOUR BIRTHPLACE.
7. DRAW A CLOCK ON THE WALL. IT IS 7:30.
8. THE BLANKET IS BROWN.

READ

GET UP

Look at the picture. Look at the woman. She is up.

Look at the man. He is not up. He is in bed.

Hey, it is 7:30 in the morning. Wake up. Open your eyes. The sun is up. Get up.

UP/DOWN

1. UP __ __ __ __   2. MAN __ __ __ __ __   3. HE __ __ __   4. OUT __ __

READ AND WRITE

GET UP

LOOK AT THE PICTURE. GET UP, BOB. OPEN _____ EYES. GO TO THE BATHROOM. WASH. DRESS. _____ BREAKFAST. GO TO WORK.

TODAY IS HERE. _____ WIFE IS UP, BOB. HEY, LISTEN, BOB, _____ UP. NOW.

I _____

_____

LISTEN AND WRITE

1: _____   A. _____

2: _____   B. _____

1: _____   C. _____

2: _____   D. _____

WRITE A NOTE

(DATE) _____

_____

(SIGNATURE) _____

COPY

i i i i

l l l

u u u

u u w w

wake up

Bob

bed

go

get

is

wash

LESSON 8   A Rainy Day

READ ALOUD

1: LOOK AT THE PICTURE.

2: OK.

1: IT'S CLOUDY.

2: RIGHT.

1: IT'S WINDY.

2: RIGHT.

1: IT'S RAINY.

2: RIGHT.

1: IT'S WET.

2: RIGHT.

1: GET YOUR UMBRELLA.

2: OK.

DIRECTIONS: LOOK AT THE PICTURE. DRAW. COLOR.

1. THE UMBRELLA ON THE RIGHT IS RED.

2. THE UMBRELLA ON THE LEFT IS YELLOW.

3. THE UMBRELLA IN THE MIDDLE IS BLUE.

4. THE BOY ON THE RIGHT HAS A GREEN RAINCOAT.

5. THE WOMAN ON THE LEFT HAS AN ORANGE RAINCOAT.

6. LOOK AT THE SIGN BEHIND THE PEOPLE. WRITE **BANK** ON THE SIGN.

READ

A BAD DAY

Look at the picture. It is cloudy. It is windy. It is rainy. It is a bad day.

Look at the people. Look at the umbrellas. Look at the raincoats.

The streets are wet. The sidewalks are wet. The umbrellas are wet. The raincoats are wet. But the people are dry.

UP/DOWN

1. DRY __ __ __   2. WRONG __ __ __ __ __   3. SUNNY __ __ __ __ __ __

READ AND WRITE

WET

I WALKED TO SCHOOL TODAY. IT RAINED. _____ AM WET. MY HAIR IS WET. _____ JACKET IS WET. MY SHOES ARE _____ . MY JEANS ARE WET. MY SOCKS _____ WET. MY BOOKS ARE WET.

I AM _____ HAPPY. MY UMBRELLA _____ HOME. STOP RAINING!

I _____

_____

LISTEN AND WRITE

1: _____   A. _____

2: _____   B. _____

1: _____   C. _____

2: _____   D. _____

WRITE A NOTE

(DATE) _____

_____

_____

_____

_____

_____

_____

(SIGNATURE) _____

COPY

t t t t

l l l

l l b b

l l h h

l l k k k

l l l b f

rainy

windy

cloudy

right   *Right*

LESSON 9　The Moon

READ ALOUD

1: LOOK AT THE PICTURE.

2: OK.

1: NIGHT.

2: RIGHT.

1: STARS.

2: RIGHT.

1: THE MOON.

2: BEAUTIFUL.

1: A FULL MOON.

2: FULL?

1: ROUND.

2: RIGHT.

DIRECTIONS: LOOK AT THE PICTURE. DRAW. COLOR.

1. THE MOON IS ORANGE.

2. THE LIGHT ON THE HOUSE IS YELLOW.

3. THE MAN HAS A RED JACKET.

4. THE MAN HAS BLACK PANTS.

5. THE HOUSE IS BROWN.

6. THE GRASS IS GREEN.

READ

THE MOON

The moon is beautiful. The moon always looks different. The moon can be full. The moon can be thin. The moon can be half size.

Look at the picture. That moon is full. That moon is round.

Go outside tonight. Look up. Look at the moon. Can you see it?

UP/DOWN

1. WOMAN _ _ _   2. WRONG _ _ _ _ _   3. DAY _ _ _ _ _

READ AND WRITE

A FULL MOON

LOOK AT THE PICTURE. LOOK AT THE _____ . THE MOON IS FULL. I LIKE _____ MOONS.

A FULL MOON IS BIG. A FULL _____ IS BRIGHT. A FULL MOON IS ROUND. A FULL MOON COMES _____ MONTH.

GO OUTSIDE TONIGHT. LOOK UP. IS THE _____ FULL?

I _____

_____

LISTEN AND WRITE

1: _____   A. _____

2: _____   B. _____

1: _____   C. _____

2: _____   D. _____

WRITE A NOTE

(DATE) _____

_____

_____

_____

_____

_____

_____

_____

(SIGNATURE) _____

COPY

(cursive practice strokes building letter m)

(cursive practice strokes building letter m)

(cursive practice strokes building letter x)

(cursive practice strokes)

(cursive practice strokes building letter y)

(cursive practice strokes building letter z)

moon   *You*

full   *you*

LESSON 10 Lock Your Door

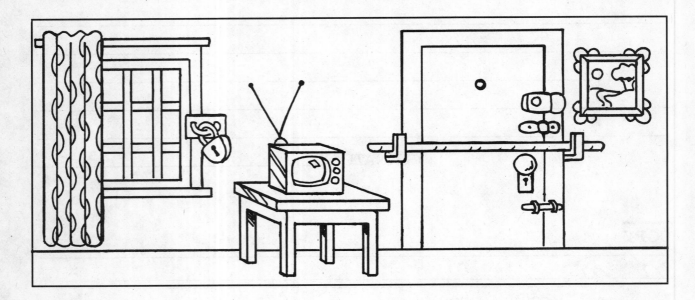

READ ALOUD

1: LOOK AT THE PICTURE.

2: WOW.

1: LOCK YOUR DOOR.

2: OK.

1: LOCK YOUR DOOR EVERY DAY.

2: OK.

1: LOCK YOUR DOOR EVERY NIGHT.

2: OK.

1: BE SAFE.

2: OK, OK.

DIRECTIONS: LOOK AT THE PICTURE. DRAW. COLOR.

1. DRAW A CLOCK ON THE WALL. IT IS 12:35.

2. THE TOP LOCK IS BLUE.

3. THE BOTTOM LOCK IS GREEN.

4. THE PADLOCK ON THE WINDOW IS RED.

5. THE TABLE IS BROWN.

6. DRAW A PICTURE IN THE FRAME. DRAW YOUR BIRTHPLACE.

7. THE PEEPHOLE IN THE DOOR IS BLACK.

READ

LOCK YOUR DOOR

Look at the picture. That is my apartment. My apartment is not safe. My apartment in the city is not safe. My apartment in the city is not safe now.

I lock my door. I lock my windows. I lock my doors and windows every day and every night.

People look at my locks and laugh, but I feel safe.

UP/DOWN

1. DANGEROUS _ _ _ _ 2. NIGHT _ _ _ 3. UNLOCK _ _ _ _ 4. OUT _ _

READ AND WRITE

SAFE OR DANGEROUS

IS YOUR HOME SAFE OR DANGEROUS? IS _____ NEIGHBORHOOD SAFE OR DANGEROUS? IS YOUR CITY _____ OR DANGEROUS?

DO YOU LOCK YOUR DOOR _____ DAY? DO YOU LOCK YOUR DOOR EVERY _____?

BE CAREFUL. LOCK YOUR DOOR. BE SAFE. ALWAYS _____ YOUR DOOR.

LISTEN AND WRITE

1: _____ A. _____

2: _____ B. _____

1: _____ C. _____

2: _____ D. _____

WRITE A NOTE

(DATE) _____

_____

_____

_____

_____

_____

_____

_____

(SIGNATURE) _____

COPY

lock   Lock

door   My

your

Be

Do

LESSON 11   Practice Pronunciation

FILL OUT

_____
(LAST NAME)   (FIRST NAME)   (MIDDLE NAME)

DATE OF BIRTH _____ - _____ - _____   COUNTRY OF BIRTH _____
            (MO)   (DAY)   (YR)

READ ALOUD

1: PRACTICE YOUR PRONUNCIATION.

2: HOW?

1: GO HOME.

2: OK.

1: GO TO THE BATHROOM.

2: OK.

1: SHUT THE DOOR.

2: OK.

1: LOOK IN THE MIRROR.

2: OK.

1: SAY, "BEAD, BID, BED, BAD."

2: OK.

1: AGAIN, AND AGAIN, AND AGAIN.

2: OK, OK.

DIRECTIONS: LOOK AT THE PICTURE. DRAW. COLOR.

1. THE MAN HAS A BLUE SHIRT.

2. THE MAN HAS BROWN PANTS.

3. DRAW THE MAN'S EYES, NOSE, AND MOUTH.

4. DRAW A PICTURE ON THE WALL.

5. DRAW A FLOWER IN THE VASE ON THE TOILET. THE FLOWER IS RED.

6. DRAW A TOOTHBRUSH ON THE SINK. THE TOOTHBRUSH IS GREEN.

7. DRAW SOAP ON THE SINK.

READ

IN THE BATHROOM

Look at the picture. Look at the mirror. Look at the man.

The man is in his bathroom. He shut the door. He is looking in the mirror. He is looking at his mouth. He is practicing his pronunciation. He is saying. "BOT, BUT, BOOT, BOAT," again, and again, and again, and again.

UP/DOWN

1. OPEN __ __ __ 2. COME __ __ 3. OUT __ __ 4. WOMAN __ __ __ 5. SHE __ __

READ AND WRITE

MIRRORS

LOOK AT THE PICTURE. LOOK AT THE MIRROR. MIRRORS _____
EVERYWHERE.

BEDROOMS HAVE MIRRORS. BATHROOMS _____ MIRRORS.
LIVING ROOMS HAVE MIRRORS. RESTAURANTS HAVE _____ .
RESTROOMS HAVE MIRRORS. STORES HAVE MIRRORS.

_____ AROUND. DOES THIS ROOM HAVE _____
MIRROR?

I _____

_____

LISTEN AND WRITE

1: _____ A. _____

2: _____ B. _____

1: _____ C. _____

2: _____ D. _____

WRITE A NOTE

(DATE) _____

_____

_____

_____

_____

_____

_____

_____

(SIGNATURE) _____

DIRECTIONS:

LOOK AT THE MAP. ASK: WHAT IS YOUR LANGUAGE? WHERE ARE YOU FROM?

WRITE THE FIRST LETTER OF THEIR LANGUAGE ON THE MAP.

EXAMPLE: 1. WHAT IS YOUR LANGUAGE?

2. SPANISH.

1. WHERE ARE YOU FROM?

2. CHILE.

1. (Writes **S** on Chile.)

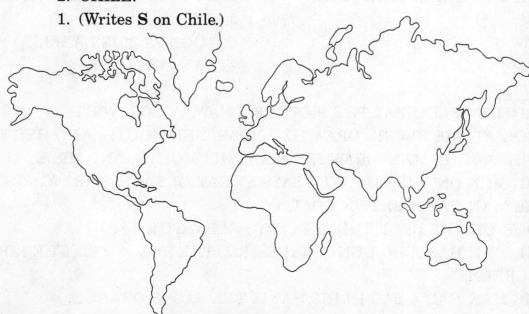

LESSON 12 Check the Label

READ ALOUD

1: ARE YOU GOING SHOPPING?

2: YES.

1: NOW?

2: YES.

1: BUY ME A SWEATER, WILL YOU?

2: OK.

1: LOOK AT THE LABEL.

2: I ALWAYS LOOK.

DIRECTIONS: LOOK AT THE PICTURE. DRAW. COLOR. WRITE.

1. LOOK AT THE CLERK. DRAW HER NOSE, HER MOUTH, AND HER EYES.

2. LOOK AT THE MAN. DRAW HIS NOSE, HIS MOUTH, AND HIS EYES.

3. THE SIGN ON THE COUNTER SAYS **SWEATER SALE**. THE SIGN IS BLUE.

4. THE MAN HAS A BROWN COAT.

5. LOOK ON THE LEFT. THE SIGN SAYS **ELEVATOR**.

6. THE MAN HAS A BOX UNDER HIS ARM. THE BOX IS RED. THE RIBBON IS GREEN.

7. THE MAN HAS A BAG IN HIS HAND. THE BAG IS ORANGE.

READ

GOOD LABELS

Look at labels. Look at labels on shirts. Look at labels on blouses. Look at labels on pants. Look at labels on underwear. Look at labels on sweaters.

Good labels show sizes. Is it small, medium, or large?

Good labels show material. Is it cotton, wool, or dacron?

Good labels show how to clean it. Can you wash it in a machine?

UP/DOWN

1. SMALL _ _ _ _ _   2. BAD _ _ _ _   3. DIRTY _ _ _ _ _   4. SELL _ _ _

READ AND WRITE

LABELS

I ALWAYS LOOK AT LABELS. I ALWAYS _____ AT THE LABEL FOR SIZE. IS IT _____ , MEDIUM, OR LARGE?

I ALWAYS LOOK AT THE _____ FOR MATERIAL. IS IT COTTON, WOOL, OR _____?

I ALWAYS LOOK AT THE LABEL FOR _____ TO CLEAN IT. CAN I WASH IT _____ A MACHINE?

LISTEN AND WRITE

1: _____   A. _____
2: _____   B. _____
1: _____   C. _____
2: _____   D. _____

WRITE A NOTE

(DATE) _____

_____

    _____

_____

_____

_____

_____

_____

(SIGNATURE) _____

DIRECTIONS:

MAKE A GOOD LABEL. LOOK AT A GOOD LABEL ON YOUR CLOTHES. COPY IT.

1. MATERIAL?
2. SIZE?
3. BRAND NAME?
4. HOW TO CLEAN IT?
5. WHERE MADE?

LESSON 13   A Holiday

FILL OUT

NAME _____

                (LAST)   (FIRST)   (MIDDLE)

SOCIAL SECURITY NUMBER _____ – _____ – _____

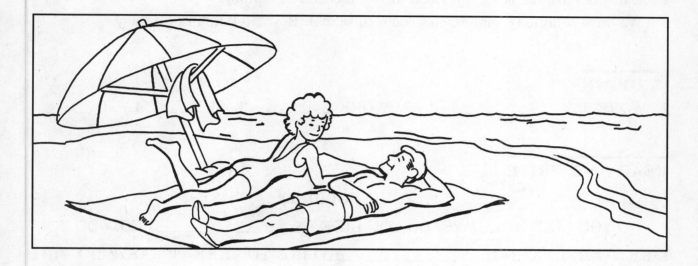

READ ALOUD

1: WE HAVE A HOLIDAY SOON.

2: OH?

1: DON'T WORK.

2: OK.

1: REST.

2: OK.

1: RELAX.

2: OK.

1: TAKE IT EASY.

2: OK, OK.

DIRECTIONS: LOOK AT THE PICTURE. DRAW. COLOR.

1. The umbrella is blue and yellow.
2. The ocean is blue.
3. The beach is brown.
4. Draw the sun in the sky.
5. The towel under the umbrella is green.
6. The man has a red bathing suit.
7. Draw a boat in the ocean.
8. The woman has a black bathing suit.
9. The man and woman are lying on an orange mat.

READ

A HOLIDAY

Look at the picture. Look at the man and woman. They have a holiday today.

They are not working. They are resting. They are relaxing. They are taking it easy.
Look at his face. He is happy. Look at her face. She is happy.

We have a holiday soon. Don't come to school. Rest. Relax. Take it easy.

UP/DOWN

1. WORKDAY _ _ _ _ _ _ _   2. WORK _ _ _ _   3. SHE _ _   4. NO _ _ _

READ AND WRITE

YOUR HOLIDAY

DO YOU LIKE HOLIDAYS? DO YOU LIKE _____ REST? DO YOU
LIKE TO RELAX? DO _____ LIKE TO TAKE IT EASY? DO YOU
_____ TO STAY HOME? YES? ME, TOO.

WE HAVE A _____ SOON. DON'T WORK. REST. RELAX. TAKE
IT _____ .

LISTEN AND WRITE

1: _____   A. _____

2: _____   B. _____

1: _____   C. _____

2: _____   D. _____

WRITE A NOTE

(DATE) _____

_____

   _____

_____

_____

_____

_____

_____

(SIGNATURE) _____

DIRECTIONS:

WRITE THE POST OFFICE ABBREVIATION OF THESE STATES ON THE MAP.

1. Write CA on California.
2. Write MA on Massachusetts.
3. Write NY on New York.
4. Write AZ on Arizona.
5. Write FL on Florida.
6. Write HA on Hawaii.
7. Write ME on Maine.
8. Write CO on Colorado.
9. Write MN on Minnesota.
10. Write IL on Illinois.
11. Write AL on Alabama.
12. Write TX on Texas.
13. Write WA on Washington.
14. Write OR on Oregon.
15. Write NM on New Mexico.
16. Write PA on Pennsylvania.
17. Write _____ on your state.

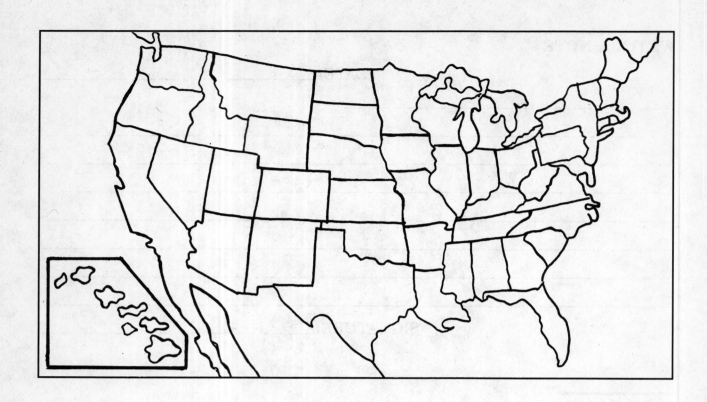

LESSON 14 The Wash

READ ALOUD

1: LOOK AT THE PICTURE.

2: OK.

1: SHE WASHED HER CLOTHES.

2: RIGHT.

1: SHE'S HANGING THEM UP.

2: RIGHT.

1: I GO TO A LAUNDROMAT.

2: ME, TOO.

DIRECTIONS: LOOK AT THE PICTURE. DRAW. COLOR.

1. THE TOWEL ON THE RIGHT IS BLUE.

2. THE TOWEL ON THE LEFT IS YELLOW.

3. THE TOWEL IN THE MIDDLE IS PINK.

4. THE WOMAN HAS A RED BLOUSE.

5. DRAW A GREEN SHIRT ON THE LINE.

6. DRAW BROWN PANTS ON THE LINE.

7. DRAW THE SUN IN THE SKY.

8. THE GRASS IS GREEN

9. DRAW A TREE BEHIND THE WOMAN.

READ

AT A LAUNDROMAT

I wash clothes at a laundromat. I wash clothes at a laundromat in my neighborhood. I wash clothes at a laundromat in my neighborhood every Saturday.

I put soap in. I put my clothes in. I put money in. I close the lid. I push a button. Then I wait, and wait, and wait.

Then I put my clothes in a dryer. Then I wait, and wait, and wait. Then I go home, and I watch TV.

UP/DOWN

1. WASH __ __ __   2. LIKE __ __ __ __   3. OPEN __ __ __ __   4. PULL __ __ __ __

READ AND WRITE

MY WASH

I HATE TO WASH CLOTHES. I HATE _____ WASH BY HAND. I HATE TO WASH _____ A WASHING MACHINE.

I HATE TO GO _____ A LAUNDROMAT. I HATE TO PUT SOAP IN. _____ HATE TO PUT MONEY IN. AND I _____ TO WAIT, AND WAIT, AND WAIT, AND _____.

BUT WHO WANTS DIRTY CLOTHES? NOT ME.

LISTEN AND WRITE

1: _____   A. _____
2: _____   B. _____
1: _____   C. _____
2: _____   D. _____

WRITE A NOTE

(DATE) _____

_____

_____

_____

_____

_____

_____

_____

(SIGNATURE) _____

DIRECTIONS:

LOOK AT THE MAP. HOW IS THE WEATHER? WHAT SHOULD YOU DO?

CLEAR ☼   / RAIN 🌧   / CLOUDY ☁   / SNOW ☁

1. WASH AND HANG OUTSIDE IN _____

2. WASH AND USE A DRYER IN _____

3. GO ON A PICNIC BY THE OCEAN IN _____

4. WEAR A RAINCOAT IN _____

5. IT IS VERY HOT. WEAR SHORTS IN _____

6. IT IS COLD. WEAR A COAT IN _____

7. TAKE AN UMBRELLA IN _____

8. GO SWIMMING IN _____

9. LOOK OUTSIDE. HOW IS THE WEATHER? _____

LESSON 15   Don't Smoke

READ ALOUD

1: THANKS.

2: WHAT?

1: THANKS FOR NOT SMOKING.

2: OK.

1: DON'T SMOKE.

2: OK.

1: NO SMOKING.

2: OK, OK.

DIRECTIONS: LOOK AT THE PICTURE. COLOR. DRAW.

1. The man has a green shirt.

2. The woman has a red dress.

3. The lamp is yellow.

4. The flowers are blue, red, and orange.

5. The man has glasses.

6. Draw a clock on the wall. It is 9:45.

7. Draw a window. Draw the moon out the window.

8. The **DON'T SMOKE** sign is red and white.

READ

SMOKING

Look at the picture. The man and woman are not smokers. They don't smoke. They don't like smoking.

Why? Smoking is expensive. Smoking is bad for people. Smoke hurts you, and smoke hurts the people near you.

UP/DOWN

1. MAN __ __ __   2. HATE __ __ __ __   3. YES __ __   4. HE __ __ __

READ AND WRITE

DON'T

I SEE **DON'T** SIGNS EVERYWHERE. I SEE **DON'T** _____ SIGNS.

I SEE **DON'T WALK** SIGNS. _____ SEE **DON'T TRESPASS** SIGNS.

I SEE **DON'T SPIT** _____. I SEE **DON'T ENTER** SIGNS. I SEE

_____ **TURN LEFT** SIGNS. I SEE **DON'T TOUCH** SIGNS.

_____ SEE **DON'T PARK** SIGNS. I SEE **DON'T LITTER**

_____. I SEE **DON'T RUN** SIGNS. I SEE _____ **SWIM**

HERE SIGNS.

LISTEN AND WRITE

1: _____   A. _____

2: _____   B. _____

1: _____   C. _____

2: _____   D. _____

WRITE A NOTE

(DATE) _____

_____

　　_____

_____

_____

_____

_____

_____

_____

(SIGNATURE) _____

DIRECTIONS:

MAKE AN INTERNATIONAL **DON'T** SIGN.

1. DON'T SMOKE.

2. DON'T TURN LEFT.

3. DON'T TURN RIGHT.

4. DON'T DRIVE A TRUCK HERE.

5. DON'T MAKE A **U** TURN.

6. DO NOT ENTER.

LESSON 16 Your Eyes

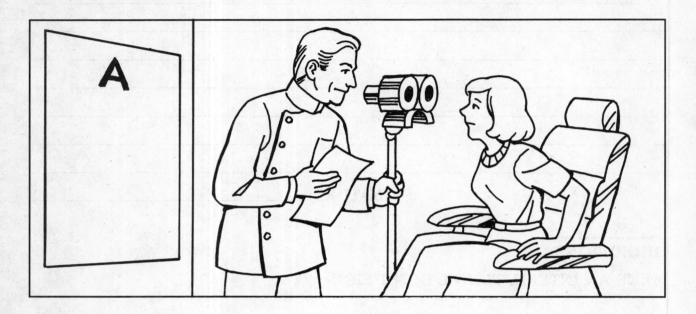

READ ALOUD

1: LOOK AT THE PICTURE.

2: OK.

1: HER EYES ARE BAD.

2: OH?

1: SHE CAN'T SEE.

2: OH?

1: THE DOCTOR IS CHECKING HER EYES.

2: I SEE.

DIRECTIONS: LOOK AT THE PICTURE. COLOR. DRAW. WRITE.

1. The woman has red jeans.
2. The doctor is holding a green piece of paper.
3. Draw a clock on the wall. It is 9:20.
4. The woman has black hair.
5. Look at the eye chart. Write **E C D F** under the big A.
6. Write a smaller **H L T M** under the E C D F.
7. Write a smaller **Z O S P** under H L T M.
8. Write a very small **X P K J** at the bottom.
9. The woman has red eyes.

READ

BAD EYES?

How are your eyes? Do your eyes hurt? Do your eyes get red? Do you get headaches?
Go to an eye doctor. Go to an eye doctor every two years. The doctor will check your eyes.
Do you wear glasses? Wear them every day.
You can't read and write if you can't see.

UP/DOWN

1. GOOD _ _ _ 2. HIS _ _ _ 3. HE _ _ _ 4. MY _ _ _ _ 5. NIGHT _ _ _

READ AND WRITE

YOUR EYES

TAKE CARE OF YOUR EYES. TAKE CARE _____ YOUR EYES AT
HOME. TAKE CARE OF _____ EYES AT SCHOOL. TAKE CARE OF
YOUR _____ AT WORK.

YOUR EYES HELP YOU. WORK IN _____ LIGHT. WEAR YOUR
GLASSES. GO TO AN EYE _____ EVERY TWO YEARS. THE DOCTOR
CAN CHECK YOUR _____.

LISTEN AND WRITE

1: _____ A. _____

2: _____ B. _____

1: _____ C. _____

2: _____ D. _____

WRITE A NOTE

(DATE) _____

_____

    _____

_____

_____

_____

_____

_____

(SIGNATURE) _____

DIRECTIONS:

LOOK AT THE MEDICINE BOTTLE LABEL.

1. THE DOCTOR'S NAME IS _____
2. THE MEDICINE IS _____
3. APPLY THE MEDICINE _____
4. THROW IT AWAY AFTER _____
5. THE NAME OF THE PATIENT IS _____
6. SHE CAN HAVE _____ MORE BOTTLES

LEE'S DRUGSTORE

Brown DR. White

TRIDESILON CREAM
APPLY TO FACE
2 TIMES DAILY

DISCARD
AFTER 6-91 REFILLS 2

MAKE A LABEL

1. YOUR DOCTOR IS DR. GREEN.
2. YOUR MEDICINE IS TENE EYE DROPS.
3. DIRECTIONS: PUT IN 2 DROPS.
4. EMPTY IT IN THE TOILET AFTER MAY, 1994.
5. YOU CAN HAVE 1 REFILL.
6. YOU ARE THE PATIENT.

LEE'S DRUGSTORE

DR. _____

DISCARD
AFTER _____ REFILLS _____

LESSON 17 In Court

READ ALOUD

1: LOOK AT THE COURT.

2: OK.

1: IS THE MAN RIGHT?

2: I DON'T KNOW.

1: IS THE MAN WRONG?

2: I DON'T KNOW.

1: OK.

2: ASK THE JUDGE.

1: OK.

DIRECTIONS: LOOK AT THE PICTURE. DRAW. COLOR. WRITE.

1. The police officer has a blue uniform and blue hat.
2. The judge has a black robe.
3. Write **JUDGE** above the judge.
4. The man has a red shirt.
5. The man has black pants.
6. Draw a clock on the wall. It is 10:20.
7. Look in the man's left hand. The ticket is yellow.
8. Draw an American flag near the judge.

READ

IN COURT

Sometimes drivers get tickets. The police officer says, "You drove too fast." The driver says, "No."

Sometimes they go to court. Look at the picture. The judge is listening. The judge will say who is right.

UP/DOWN

1. RIGHT _ _ _ _   2. WOMAN _ _ _   3. FAR _ _ _ _

READ AND WRITE

RIGHT OR WRONG

LOOK AT THE PICTURE, LOOK AT THE COURTROOM. _____ AT THE MAN. LOOK AT THE POLICE OFFICER. LOOK _____ THE JUDGE. THE JUDGE IS LISTENING.

IS THE _____ RIGHT OR WRONG? IS THE POLICE OFFICER _____ OR WRONG?

I DON'T KNOW. ASK THE _____.

LISTEN AND WRITE

1: _____   A. _____
2: _____   B. _____
1: _____   C. _____
2: _____   D. _____

WRITE A NOTE

(DATE) _____

_____

_____

_____

_____

_____

_____

_____

_____

(SIGNATURE) _____

DIRECTIONS:

Sometimes people pay a fine by mail. Write a check. Address an envelope. Your fine is
$20.00. Make the check out to TRAFFIC COURT. Send the check to HALL OF JUSTICE,
901 BRIAN STREET, SAN FRANCISCO, CA 94103.

_____ 19 ____

Pay _____ $ _____

_____ DOLLARS

_____

_____

_____

_____

_____

_____

LESSON 18   Who Cooks?

READ ALOUD

1: YOU ARE COOKING TONIGHT.   1: 50–50.

2: RIGHT.   2: I LOVE YOU.

1: I AM COOKING TOMORROW.

2: OK.

DIRECTIONS: LOOK AT THE PICTURE. DRAW. COLOR. WRITE.

1. THE WOMAN HAS A RED APRON.

2. THE WOMAN HAS BLUE PANTS.

3. THE MAN HAS A GREEN SHIRT.

4. THE MAN HAS BLACK PANTS.

5. THE MIXING BOWL IS ORANGE.

6. DRAW A CLOCK ON THE WALL. IT IS 6:15.

7. THE REFRIGERATOR IS BROWN.

8. THE BOX ON THE REFRIGERATOR IS RED.

READ

50–50

In many families the wife works and the husband works. They are both tired at night.

Now, in many families, sometimes the wife cooks. Sometimes the husband cooks. Sometimes the wife vacuums. Sometimes the husband vacuums. Sometimes the wife washes dishes. Sometimes the husband washes dishes. Sometimes the wife washes clothes. Sometimes the husband washes clothes.

It's 50-50.

UP/DOWN

1. DAY _ _ _ _ _   2. I _ _ _   3. WOMAN _ _ _   4. WRONG _ _ _ _ _

READ AND WRITE

WHO?

WHO COOKS IN YOUR FAMILY? WHO PAYS _____ BILLS IN YOUR FAMILY? WHO VACUUMS IN _____ FAMILY? WHO WASHES DISHES IN YOUR FAMILY? _____ WASHES CLOTHES IN YOUR FAMILY? WHO SHOPS _____ YOUR FAMILY? WHO FIXES THINGS IN YOUR _____? WHO TAKES CARE OF THE KIDS IN _____ FAMILY?

IS IT 50-50?

LISTEN AND WRITE

1: _____   A. _____
2: _____   B. _____
1: _____   C. _____
2: _____   D. _____

WRITE A NOTE

(DATE) _____

_____

  _____

_____

_____

_____

_____

_____

(SIGNATURE) _____

DIRECTIONS:

WHO CLEANS IN YOUR HOME? YOU? YOUR HUSBAND? YOUR WIFE? YOUR SON? YOUR DAUGHTER? YOUR ROOMMATE?

	Me	My ___	My ___	My friend's ___	My friend's ___
Cooks					
Breakfast	___	___	___	___	___
Lunch	___	___	___	___	___
Dinner	___	___	___	___	___
Washes dishes	___	___	___	___	___
Washes clothes	___	___	___	___	___
Sweeps	___	___	___	___	___
Cleans toilet	___	___	___	___	___
Makes bed	___	___	___	___	___
Empties garbage	___	___	___	___	___
Buys food	___	___	___	___	___
Vacuums	___	___	___	___	___
Dusts	___	___	___	___	___
Sets the table	___	___	___	___	___
Gardens	___	___	___	___	___

LESSON 19 Small Stores

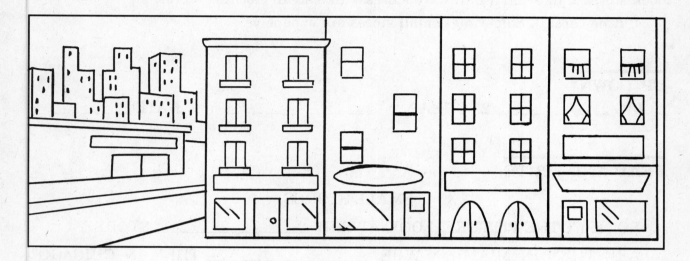

READ ALOUD

1: LOOK AT THE PICTURE.

2: OK.

1: I SEE SMALL STORES.

2: RIGHT.

1: A HARDWARE STORE.

2: RIGHT.

1: A GROCERY STORE.

2: RIGHT.

1: A SHOE STORE.

2: RIGHT.

1: A DRUGSTORE.

2: RIGHT.

1: I LIKE SMALL STORES.

2: ME, TOO.

DIRECTIONS: LOOK AT THE PICTURE. DRAW. COLOR. WRITE.

1. ONE STORE IS LEE'S GROCERY STORE.

2. ONE STORE IS A DRUGSTORE.

3. ONE STORE IS A SHOE STORE.

4. ONE STORE IS A HARDWARE STORE.

5. THE DRUGSTORE IS BROWN.

6. THE SHOE STORE IS GREEN.

7. THE HARDWARE STORE IS RED.

8. LEE'S GROCERY STORE IS BLUE.

9. DRAW THE SUN IN THE SKY.

Lesson 19 / 57

READ

SMALL STORES

I like small stores. I don't like big stores.

I like small grocery stores. I like small drugstores. I like small shoe stores. I like small book stores. I like small hardware stores. I like small clothing stores.

But be careful. Sometimes small stores are expensive.

UP/DOWN

1. BIG _ _ _ _ _   2. CHEAP _ _ _ _ _ _ _ _ _   3. HATE _ _ _ _

READ AND WRITE

SMALL STORES

LOOK AT THE PICTURE. LOOK AT THE _____ STORES.

ARE THEY IN MIAMI? MAYBE. _____ THEY IN CHICAGO? MAYBE. ARE THEY IN LOS ANGELES? _____ . ARE THEY IN NEW YORK? MAYBE. ARE _____ IN VANCOUVER? MAYBE. ARE THEY IN _____? MAYBE. ARE THEY IN NEW ORLEANS? MAYBE. ARE THEY _____ THIS CITY? MAYBE.

LISTEN AND WRITE

1: _____   A. _____

2: _____   B. _____

1: _____   C. _____

2: _____   D. _____

WRITE A NOTE

(DATE) _____

_____

　　_____

_____

_____

_____

_____

_____

_____

(SIGNATURE) _____

DIRECTIONS:

DRAW A MAP. SHOW YOUR HOME. NAME STREETS. NAME STORES. WRITE
NORTH AT THE TOP. WRITE **SOUTH** AT THE BOTTOM. WRITE **EAST** ON THE
RIGHT. WRITE **WEST** ON THE LEFT.

_____

_____   _____

_____

LESSON 20 A Fight

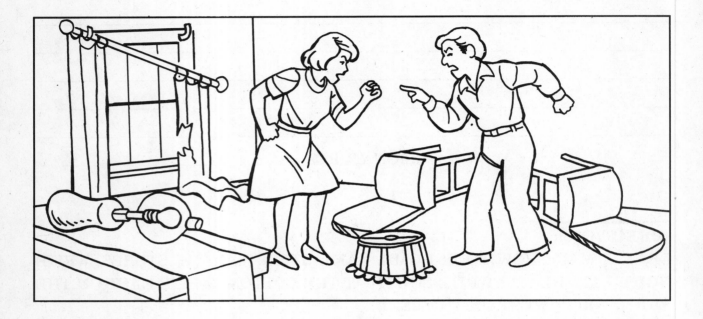

READ ALOUD

1: YOU SPEND TOO MUCH MONEY.

2: NO, I DON'T. (CRASH)

1: YES, YOU DO. (BANG)

2: NO, I DON'T. (BOOM)

1: YES, YOU DO. (POW)

2: WRONG, WRONG, WRONG.

1: RIGHT, RIGHT, RIGHT.

DIRECTIONS: LOOK AT THE PICTURE. DRAW. COLOR.

1. The woman has a blue blouse.
2. The woman has a yellow skirt.
3. The man has a green shirt.
4. The man has brown pants.
5. The lamp is orange.
6. The drapes are red.
7. Draw a clock on the wall. It is broken. It is 10:30.
8. Draw a picture on the wall. It is broken.

READ

FAMILY FIGHTS

Families argue. Husbands say NO. Wives say YES. Mothers and fathers say YES. Children say NO. Why?

Mothers and fathers argue about their children. Husbands and wives argue about money. Husbands and wives argue about love. Husbands and wives argue about cleaning and cooking. Children argue about toys.

Look at the picture. Many things are broken. Not many families argue like that.

UP/DOWN

1. WIVES _ _ _ _ _ _ _ 　　2. NO _ _ _ 　　3. AGREE _ _ _ _ _

READ AND WRITE

WHY PEOPLE FIGHT

PEOPLE FIGHT. LOOK AT THE PICTURE. THE _____ AND WOMAN ARE FIGHTING.

PEOPLE FIGHT ABOUT MONEY. _____ FIGHT ABOUT CHILDREN. PEOPLE FIGHT ABOUT FOOD. PEOPLE _____ ABOUT WORK AROUND THE HOME.

DO _____ FIGHT AT HOME? WHAT DO YOU _____ ABOUT?

LISTEN AND WRITE

1: _____ A. _____
2: _____ B. _____
1: _____ C. _____
2: _____ D. _____

WRITE A NOTE

(DATE) _____

_____

_____

_____

_____

_____

_____

_____

(SIGNATURE)_____

MAKE A BUDGET

Families argue about money. How much do we spend on food, on rent, on health?

Paycheck   Rent $400 🏠   Bus $28 🚐   Doctor $20 ✚   Phone $10 ☎
$644.00   Food $160 🥕 Movie $6 📺 Clothes $15 👕   Save $5

MAKE YOUR BUDGET

LESSON 21 Lost and Found

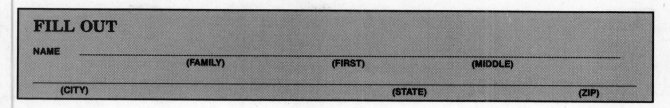

FILL OUT

NAME _____
                   (FAMILY)   (FIRST)   (MIDDLE)

    (CITY)   (STATE)   (ZIP)

READ ALOUD

1: HEY.

2: WHAT?

1: I LOST MY MONEY.

2: GO TO LOST AND FOUND.

1: I LOST MY KEYS.

2: GO TO LOST AND FOUND.

1: I LOST MY BOOK.

2: GO TO LOST AND FOUND.

1: OK, OK.

DIRECTIONS: LOOK AT THE PICTURE. DRAW. COLOR. WRITE.

1. Write **LOST AND FOUND** above the counter.

2. The **LOST AND FOUND** sign is red and black.

3. Draw a clock on the wall. The time is 2:45.

4. Write **OPEN 9:00 to 5:00** on the sign on the counter.

5. Draw the clerk's eyes, nose, ears, and mouth.

6. The customer has glasses.

7. The clerk has a yellow shirt.

8. The customer has a blue jacket.

READ

LOST AND FOUND

Mary is lucky. She lost her umbrella, but she found it. She lost her money, but she found it. She lost her book, but she found it. She lost her pen, but she found it. She lost her key, but she found it.

How? She went to **LOST AND FOUND**.

UP/DOWN

1. LOST __ __ __ __   2. FIND __ __ __   3. HIS __ __ __   4. YOUR __ __   5. YOU __

READ AND WRITE

LOST AND FOUND

DID YOU LOSE YOUR KEY? GO TO _____ AND FOUND. DID YOU

LOSE YOUR MONEY? _____ TO LOST AND FOUND. DID YOU LOSE

_____ BOOK? GO TO LOST AND FOUND. DID _____

LOSE YOUR UMBRELLA? GO TO LOST AND _____. DID YOU LOSE

YOUR WATCH? GO TO LOST _____ FOUND. DID YOU LOSE YOUR

_____? GO TO LOST AND FOUND.

I _____

_____

LISTEN AND WRITE

1: _____   A. _____

2: _____   B. _____

1: _____   C. _____

2: _____   D. _____

WRITE A NOTE

(DATE) _____

_____

   _____

_____

_____

_____

_____

_____

(SIGNATURE) _____

DIRECTIONS:

BIG STORES HAVE DIRECTORIES. MAKE A DIRECTORY. WRITE THE DEPART-
MENT ON THE FLOOR. ARRANGE ALPHABETICALLY.

A-B-C-D-E-F-G-H-I-J-K-L-M-N-O-P-Q-R-S-T-U-V-W-X-Y-Z

REST ROOMS	LOST AND FOUND	APPLIANCES
1st floor	Basement	Basement
WOMEN'S SHOES	TV	CUSTOMER SERVICE
2nd floor	2nd floor	1st floor
TOYS	MEN'S SUITS	SPORTS
2nd floor	1st floor	Basement
DRESSES	RADIOS	RESTAURANT
2nd floor	2nd floor	Basement

BASEMENT	FIRST FLOOR	SECOND FLOOR
_____	_____	_____
_____	_____	_____
_____	_____	_____
_____	_____	_____

LESSON 22   Shake Hands

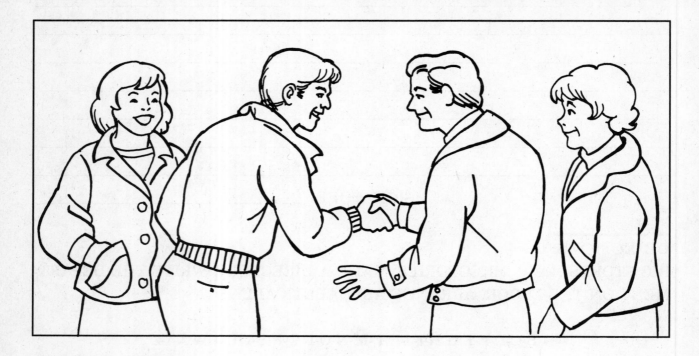

READ ALOUD

1: I GOT MARRIED YESTERDAY.   1: THANKS.

2: WOW. CONGRATULATIONS.   2: SHAKE.

                                              1: THANKS.

DIRECTIONS: LOOK AT THE PICTURE. DRAW. COLOR. WRITE.

1. The man on the right has a green jacket.
2. The man on the left has a blue jacket.
3. The woman on the left has a red jacket.
4. The woman on the right has a yellow jacket.
5. Draw the moon in the sky.
6. The woman in the red jacket has glasses.
7. The woman in the yellow jacket has a hat.
8. Write **49ers** on the back of the blue jacket.
9. Write **GIANTS** on the back of the green jacket.

READ

SHAKE HANDS

Look at the picture. The men are friends. They are shaking hands.

People shake hands when they meet. People shake hands when they say goodbye. People shake hands when a friend gets a new job. People shake hands when a friend gets married. People shake hands when a friend graduates from school.

Sometimes people hug. Sometimes people kiss on the cheek.

What do you do?

UP/DOWN

1. ENEMY _ _ _ _ _ _   2. HELLO _ _ _ _ _ _ _ _   3. WOMEN _ _ _

READ AND WRITE

SHAKE MY HAND

BE MY FRIEND. SHAKE MY HAND. PEOPLE _____ HANDS IN

MANY COUNTRIES. PEOPLE SHAKE HANDS _____ THE U.S.A.

PEOPLE SHAKE HANDS IN CANADA. _____ SHAKE HANDS IN

ENGLAND. PEOPLE SHAKE HANDS IN _____. PEOPLE SHAKE

HANDS IN AUSTRALIA. PEOPLE SHAKE _____ IN MEXICO.

PEOPLE SHAKE HANDS IN NEW ZEALAND.

DO _____ SHAKE HANDS IN YOUR NATIVE COUNTRY?

LISTEN AND WRITE

1: _____ A. _____

2: _____ B. _____

1: _____ C. _____

2: _____ D. _____

WRITE A NOTE

(DATE) _____

_____

_____

_____

_____

_____

_____

_____

(SIGNATURE) _____

DIRECTIONS:

YOU ARE BUYING A USED CAR FROM TIM WALSH. YOU GIVE TIM A CHECK FOR $1,000. (ONE THOUSAND DOLLARS). YOU SHAKE HANDS.

_____ 19 _____

PAY TO THE
ORDER OF _____ $ [_____]

_____ DOLLARS

_____

LESSON 23 A Family Tree

FILL OUT

NAME _____

               (FAMILY)   (FIRST)   (MIDDLE)

COUNTRY OF BIRTH _____ COLOR OF EYES _____

READ ALOUD

1: LOOK AT THE PICTURE.
2: OK.
1: THE WHOLE FAMILY.
2: WOW.
1: GRANDMOTHER AND GRANDFATHER.
2: IN THE MIDDLE.

1: FATHER AND MOTHER.
2: ON THE LEFT.
1: SON AND DAUGHTER.
2: ON THE RIGHT.
1: RIGHT.

DIRECTIONS: LOOK AT THE PICTURE. COLOR. DRAW.

1. THE FATHER HAS A BLUE BATHING SUIT.
2. THE MOTHER HAS A BLACK BATHING SUIT.
3. THE SON HAS A GREEN BATHING SUIT.
4. THE DAUGHTER HAS A YELLOW BATHING SUIT.
5. THE GRANDFATHER HAS AN ORANGE SHIRT.
6. THE GRANDMOTHER HAS A PINK DRESS.
7. THE BEACH UMBRELLA IS PURPLE AND GOLD.
8. THE SAND IS BROWN.
9. THE KITE IS RED.
10. THE OCEAN IS BLUE.

READ

A FAMILY

My family lives in one apartment. My grandmother and my grandfather, my son and my daughter, my wife and I live together.

It is crowded. The living room is a bedroom. The dining room is a bedroom. The kitchen is the dining room.

Never mind. Rents are high. Our rent is so-so. We will move some day. But for now, it is OK.

UP/DOWN

1. LOW _ _ _ _   2. FATHER _ _ _ _ _ _   3. SON _ _ _ _ _ _ _ _

READ AND WRITE

FAMILIES

FAMILIES ARE ALL DIFFERENT. SOME FAMILIES ARE _____.
SOME FAMILIES ARE SMALL. SOME FAMILIES ARE MEDIUM SIZED.

_____ FAMILIES HAVE ALL BOYS. SOME FAMILIES

_____ ALL GIRLS. SOME FAMILIES HAVE BOYS

_____ GIRLS.

SOME FAMILIES ARE FRIENDLY. SOME FAMILIES FIGHT. _____
FAMILIES HELP EACH OTHER. SOME FAMILIES DON'T _____ EACH
OTHER.

TELL ME ABOUT YOUR _____.

LISTEN AND WRITE

1: _____   A. _____

2: _____   B. _____

1: _____   C. _____

2: _____   D. _____

WRITE A NOTE

(DATE) _____

_____

   _____

_____

_____

_____

_____

_____

_____

(SIGNATURE) _____

MY FAMILY TREE:

MY WIFE IS LEE.

MY SON IS JOE.

OUR DAUGHTER IS JANE.

JOE'S AND JANE'S UNCLE IS KIM.

JOE'S AND JANE'S AUNT IS KATE.

LEE'S MOTHER IS BETTY.

MY FATHER IS BOB.

GRANDMOTHER/_____   _____/GRANDFATHER

ME   LEE

YOUR FAMILY TREE:

LESSON 24 Mail

READ ALOUD

1: HEY.

2: WHAT?

1: MAIL MY LETTER.

2: PLEASE.

1: OK, OK. PLEASE MAIL MY LETTER.

2: OK.

DIRECTIONS: LOOK AT THE PICTURE. DRAW. COLOR.

1. The mailbox is blue.
2. Write **U.S. MAIL** on the mailbox.
3. The girl has a green and blue scarf.
4. The girl has a red jacket.
5. The girl has an orange hat.
6. The girl has brown pants.
7. Draw a car behind the girl. The car is yellow.
8. Draw a street sign behind the girl. It is **MAIN ST.**

READ

NO LETTER

I look for a letter every day. I wait for a letter every day. I pray for a letter every day. But no letter.

How is my family? I don't know. Where is my family? I don't know. How are my friends? I don't know. Where are my friends? I don't know.

I just wait, and look, and wait, and hope.

UP/DOWN

1. NIGHT _ _ _   2. YOUR _ _   3. ENEMY _ _ _ _ _ _   4. YOU _

READ AND WRITE

HOW MUCH MAIL

HOW MUCH MAIL DO YOU GET? DO _____ GET ONE LETTER A DAY? DO YOU _____ ONE LETTER A WEEK? DO YOU GET _____ LETTER A MONTH? DO YOU GET ONE _____ A YEAR?

HOW MANY LETTERS DO YOU _____? DO YOU WRITE ONE LETTER A DAY? _____ YOU WRITE ONE LETTER A WEEK? DO _____ WRITE ONE LETTER A MONTH? DO YOU _____ ONE LETTER A YEAR?

I _____

_____

LISTEN AND WRITE

1: _____   A. _____

2: _____   B. _____

1: _____   C. _____

2: _____   D. _____

WRITE A NOTE

(DATE) _____

_____

_____

_____

_____

_____

_____

_____

(SIGNATURE) _____

DIRECTIONS:

When you move, go to the Post Office. Get a CHANGE OF ADDRESS REQUEST. Change your address.

Fill out this CHANGE OF ADDRESS REQUEST. Your new address is:

1234 Main Street Apt. 201

San Francisco, CA 95678

As soon as you know your new address, mail this card to all of the people, businesses, and publications who send you mail.

For publications, tape an old address label over name and old address sections and complete new address.

Your Name (Print or type. Last name, first name, middle initial.)					
Old Address No. & Street	Apt./Suite No.	PO Box	RR No.	Rural Box No.	
Old Address City	State	ZIP + 4			
New Address No. & Street	Apt./Suite No.	PO Box	RR No.	Rural Box No.	
New Address City	State	ZIP + 4			
Sign Here	Date new address in effect	Keyline No. (If any)			

PS Form **3576**, August 1989   RECEIVER: Be sure to record the above new address.

LESSON 25 Late for the Doctor

READ ALOUD

1: LOOK AT THE TWO PICTURES.
2: OK.
1: THE MAN IS SLEEPING.
2: RIGHT.
1: THE DOCTOR IS WAITING.
2: RIGHT.

1: THE MAN IS LATE.
2: RIGHT.
1: OH, OH.
2: RIGHT.

DIRECTIONS: LOOK AT THE PICTURE. DRAW. COLOR.

1. The doctor has black pants.
2. The nurse on the left has yellow hair.
3. The nurse on the right has red hair.
4. Draw a clock on the wall in the picture on the right. It is 9:15.
5. Draw a picture on the wall in the picture on the right.
6. Look at the picture on the left. The blanket is blue.
7. Look at the picture on the left. The sheets are green.

READ

SICK?

Are you sick? Go to bed. Are you very sick? Call the doctor. Make an appointment. Write the time of the appointment. Write the date of the appointment. Write the doctor's name. Write the doctor's office number.

Go early.

UP/DOWN

1. LATE __ __ __ __ __ 2. WRONG __ __ __ __ __ 3. HE __ __ __ 4. LAST __ __ __ __ __

READ AND WRITE

AN APPOINTMENT

ARE YOU SICK? CALL THE DOCTOR. MAKE _____ APPOINTMENT.

ASK THE DOCTOR'S NAME. WRITE _____. ASK THE DOCTOR'S OFFICE NUMBER. WRITE IT. _____ THE DATE. WRITE IT. ASK _____ TIME. WRITE IT.

GO TO YOUR _____ EARLY. TAKE THE DOCTOR'S NAME WITH YOU. _____ THE DOCTOR'S OFFICE NUMBER WITH YOU. TAKE THE _____ TELEPHONE NUMBER WITH YOU. TAKE _____ DATE WITH YOU. TAKE THE TIME WITH _____.

LISTEN AND WRITE

1: _____ A. _____

2: _____ B. _____

1: _____ C. _____

2: _____ D. _____

WRITE A NOTE

(DATE) _____

_____.

_____

_____

_____

_____

_____

_____

(SIGNATURE) _____

DIRECTIONS:

LOOK AT THE APPOINTMENT CARD. WRITE.

1. YOUR APPOINTMENT IS FOR 4:00 P.M.
2. YOUR APPOINTMENT IS FOR MONDAY, JULY 19th.
3. YOUR APPOINTMENT IS FOR DR. BROWN.
4. YOUR APPOINTMENT IS IN ROOM 301.

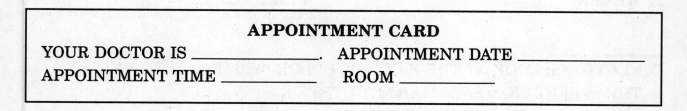

APPOINTMENT CARD

YOUR DOCTOR IS _____. APPOINTMENT DATE _____
APPOINTMENT TIME _____ ROOM _____

DIRECTIONS:

LOOK AT THE THERMOMETERS. COLOR THE TEMPERATURE RED.

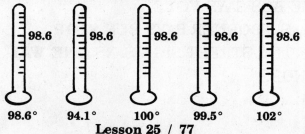

98.6°   94.1°   100°   99.5°   102°

LESSON 26 Signs

READ ALOUD

1: SIGNS, SIGNS, SIGNS.
2: WHERE?

1: EVERYWHERE.
2: I LIKE SIGNS.
1: OK, OK.

DIRECTIONS: LOOK AT THE PICTURE. COLOR. WRITE.

1. THE STREET SIGN SAYS **MARKET STREET.**
2. THE WALK SIGN SAYS **DON'T WALK.**
3. THE BUS IS THE **47 NOE.**
4. THE STORE SIGN SAYS **SEARS.**
5. THE SIGN ON THE BUS SAYS **VOTE.**
6. THE SIGN NEAR THE CORNER SAYS **BUS STOP.**
7. THE SIGN ABOVE THE STREET SIGN SAYS **ONE WAY.**
8. THE BUS IS ORANGE.
9. THE CAR IS BLUE.

READ

SIGNS

Signs are everywhere. Signs are in school. Signs are on the street. Signs are in the Post Office. Signs are in stores. Signs are on buses. Signs are on street cars. Signs are on taxis. Signs are on buildings. Signs are on freeways.

Signs say **DON'T WALK.** Signs say **ONE WAY.** Signs say **BUS STOP.** Signs, signs, signs.

UP/DOWN

1. OUT __ __   2. HATE __ __ __   3. GO __ __ __   4. BIG __ __ __ __

READ AND WRITE

SIGNS

I LIKE SIGNS. I LIKE BIG SIGNS. _____ LIKE SMALL SIGNS. I LIKE TALL SIGNS. I _____ SHORT SIGNS. I LIKE SQUARE SIGNS. I LIKE _____ SIGNS.

I LIKE RED SIGNS. I LIKE _____ SIGNS. I LIKE GREEN SIGNS. I LIKE YELLOW _____.

I LIKE PEOPLE ON SIGNS. I LIKE _____ ON SIGNS. I LIKE TREES ON SIGNS. _____ LIKE FOOD ON SIGNS.

WOW! SIGNS ARE _____.

LISTEN AND WRITE

1: _____   A. _____
2: _____   B. _____
1: _____   C. _____
2: _____   D. _____

WRITE A NOTE

(DATE) _____

_____

_____

_____

_____

_____

_____

_____

_____

(SIGNATURE) _____

DIRECTIONS:

MAKE A SIGN.

1. Write **STOP** on the sign.

2. Write **EXIT** on the sign.

3. Write **ENTRANCE** on the sign.

LESSON 27   A Crowded Bus

READ ALOUD

1: LOOK AT THE PICTURE.

2: OK.

1: THAT'S MY BUS.

2: WOW.

1: IT'S CROWDED.

2: WOW.

1: EVERY DAY.

2: WOW.

DIRECTIONS: LOOK AT THE PICTURE. DRAW. WRITE. COLOR.

1. The cowboy hat is brown.

2. The woman's big hat is yellow.

3. The baseball cap is red.

4. The stocking hat is blue.

5. The hardhat is orange.

6. The wool cap is black.

7. The man's felt hat is green.

8. Above the window draw a tube of toothpaste. Write **BRUSH WITH TOOTHPASTE**.

READ

A TRANSFER

Look at the picture. That is one of my buses. I take two buses to school. I pay my money on the first bus. I say, "Transfer, please."

I don't pay on the second bus. I give the driver my transfer.

It's easy. It's cheap.

UP/DOWN

1. EXPENSIVE _ _ _ _   2. NIGHT _ _ _   3. YOUR _ _

READ AND WRITE

CROWDED

EVERYTHING IS CROWDED IN THIS CITY. _____ ARE CROWDED. STORES ARE CROWDED. MOVIES ARE CROWDED. BUILDINGS _____ CROWDED. SCHOOLS ARE CROWDED. STREETS ARE _____. POST OFFICES ARE CROWDED. BANKS ARE CROWDED. PARKS _____ CROWDED.

I DON'T LIKE CROWDS. I DON'T _____ A LOT OF PEOPLE.

I _____

_____

LISTEN AND WRITE

1: _____   A. _____

2: _____   B. _____

1: _____   C. _____

2: _____   D. _____

WRITE A NOTE

(DATE) _____

_____

_____

_____

_____

_____

_____

_____

_____

(SIGNATURE) _____

DIRECTIONS:

Make a LIFE LINE. Look at Kim's life line.

1961	1967	1970	1976	1976	1978	1978	1980	1982
Born	School	War	Leave country	Refugee camp	Come to U.S.	Study English	Marry	Baby

YOUR LIFE LINE:

19_____

Born _____

19_____

LESSON 28   TV

READ ALOUD

1: LOOK AT THE PICTURE.

2: OK. I'M LOOKING.

1: HE WATCHED TV ALL NIGHT.

2: WOW.

1: HE SAT THERE ALL NIGHT.

2: WOW.

1: HE DRANK ALL NIGHT.

2: WOW.

1: HE ATE ALL NIGHT.

2: WOW.

1: HE'S SLEEPY NOW.

2: RIGHT.

DIRECTIONS: LOOK AT THE PICTURE. DRAW. COLOR.

1. The man has red eyes.

2. The man has a yellow shirt.

3. The man has green pants.

4. The sun is orange.

5. The TV set is brown.

6. The TV legs are black.

7. The chair is blue.

8. The clouds are red.

9. Draw a clock on the wall. It is 6:45.

READ

ALL NIGHT

Look at the picture. Look at the man. He watched TV all night. He sat in his chair all night. He drank all night. He ate popcorn all night.

Look at his eyes. They are red. Wow.

UP/DOWN

1. NONE __ __ __ 2. WOMAN __ __ __ 3. DAY __ __ __ __ __ 4. WRONG __ __ __ __ __

READ AND WRITE

TV

DO YOU HAVE TV? DO _____ LIKE TV? DO YOU WATCH TV? DO YOU WATCH _____ EVERY NIGHT?

DO YOU WATCH CHANNEL 2? _____ YOU WATCH CHANNEL 4? DO YOU WATCH _____ 7? DO YOU WATCH CHANNEL _____?

DO YOU WATCH THE NEWS ON TV? _____ YOU WATCH GAMES ON TV? DO YOU WATCH _____ ON TV?

LISTEN AND WRITE

1: _____ A. _____

2: _____ B. _____

1: _____ C. _____

2: _____ D. _____

WRITE A NOTE

(DATE) _____

_____

_____

_____

_____

_____

_____

(SIGNATURE) _____

DIRECTIONS:

LOOK AT THE TV GUIDE. WRITE ON THE GUIDE.

1. Write **MONDAY PRIME TIME** at the top.
2. Write **6:30**.
3. Write **8:00**.
4. 6:00 to 8:00 Channel 4 **MOVIE: THE GODFATHER**
5. 8:00 Channel 7 **LISTEN**
6. 6:00 Channel 5 **NEWS**
7. 7:00 to 8:30 Channel 9 **FOOTBALL**
8. 7:00 Channel 2 **ANIMALS**
9. 7:30 Channel 2 **BUSINESS**

Channel	6:00	_____	7:00	7:30	_____
2	Women	Rip Off	_____	_____	Special
4	Movie: _____				Money
5	_____	Doctor Lee	Take It	New Books	Your Credit
7	Win It	Family	For Kids	Who?	_____
9	Tell Me	Call In	_____		

LESSON 29 At The Supermarket

READ ALOUD

1: LOOK AT THE PICTURE.

2: OK.

1: HE'S IN A SUPERMARKET.

2: RIGHT.

1: HE HAS HIS MONEY.

2: RIGHT.

1: HE HAS HIS LIST.

2: RIGHT.

1: HE HAS HIS CART.

2: RIGHT.

1: BUY, MAN, BUY.

DIRECTIONS: LOOK AT THE PICTURE. DRAW. COLOR. WRITE.

1. The aisle on the left is aisle 1.

2. The aisle on the left has RICE and FLOUR.

3. The aisle in the middle is aisle 2.

4. The aisle in the middle has VEGETABLES.

5. The aisle on the right is aisle 3.

6. The aisle on the right has FRUIT.

7. The man has a blue jacket.

READ

SUPERMARKETS

Look at the picture. The man is shopping in a supermarket. He has his shopping list. He has his cart. He's going to aisle 3. He wants fruit.

We need food, too. Come on. Get your money. Get your shopping list. Let's go to the supermarket.

UP/DOWN

1. WOMAN _ _ _ 2. RIGHT _ _ _ _ 3. COME _ _ 4. SHE _ _ 5. OUT _ _

READ AND WRITE

MAKE A LIST

ARE YOU GOING TO THE SUPERMARKET? MAKE _____ LIST. MAKE A LIST OF VEGETABLES. MAKE A _____ OF FRUIT. MAKE A LIST OF DRINKS. _____ A LIST OF MEAT.

IS TEA ON _____ LIST? NO? DON'T BUY IT. IS MILK _____ YOUR LIST? NO? DON'T BUY IT. IS _____ ON YOUR LIST? NO? DON'T BUY IT.

_____ RICE ON YOUR LIST? YES? OK, BUY _____.

LISTEN AND WRITE   **MY LIST**

1: _____   A. _____

2: _____   B. _____

1: _____   C. _____

2: _____   D. _____

WRITE A NOTE

(DATE) _____

_____

_____

_____

_____

_____

_____

_____

(SIGNATURE) _____

DIRECTIONS:

LOOK AT THE GROUND BEEF PREMIUM LABEL.

1. WHAT IS THE PRICE PER POUND? _____

2. WHAT IS THE NET WEIGHT? _____

3. WHAT IS THE TOTAL PRICE? _____

```
┌─────────────────────────────────────────────────────┐
│              GROUND BEEF PREMIUM                       │
│                                                        │
│                                        ┌────────────┐  │
│   6-18-91    $3.59          1/4        │TOTAL PRICE │  │
│  ─────────────────────────────────    ├────────────┤  │
│                                        │ $  .89     │  │
│    DATE       PRICE/LB.    NET WT. LB. └────────────┘  │
└─────────────────────────────────────────────────────┘
```

LOOK AT THE FRYING CHICKEN.

1. THE TOTAL PRICE IS $2.43.

2. THE PRICE IS $0.59 PER POUND.

3. THE WEIGHT IS 4.12.

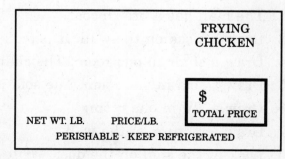

LESSON 30   For Rent

READ ALOUD

1: LOOK AT THAT APARTMENT.
2: OK.
1: WHERE ARE THE CHAIRS?
2: I DON'T KNOW.
1: WHERE IS THE SOFA?
2: I DON'T KNOW.

1: WHERE IS THE TV?
2: I DON'T KNOW.
1: WAIT A MINUTE.
2: OK.
1: IT'S FOR RENT.
2: MAYBE.

DIRECTIONS: LOOK AT THE PICTURE. DRAW. COLOR. WRITE.

1. The woman has a red dress.
2. The man has a brown coat.
3. Draw a clock on the wall. It is 5:55.
4. Draw a chair in one room. The chair is green.
5. Draw a sofa in one room. The sofa is black.
6. Draw a TV in one room.
7. Draw a picture on the wall.
8. Look at the sign on the door. Write **FOR RENT** on the sign.

READ

FOR RENT

1. Which apartment is $550? <u>C</u>
2. Which apartment has a stove? __
3. Which apartment has wall to wall carpets? __
4. Which apartment has a garage? __
5. Which apartment is sunny? __
6. Which apartment has a laundry? __
7. Which apartment has a fee? __

A. $450 studio, grg. no pets, deck, redec., nr. trans. after 5: 661−2234.

B. $725 sunny, 4rms. stv/frig. garb pd. 445−5566.

C. $550 Vw. 1BR, utilities pd. nr park hrdwd flrs. laund. Fee. 667−1213.

D. $650−700 Attrac. 3 rms, 2 wall beds, w/w cpt. Call 444−7271.

READ AND WRITE

HOW MUCH IS THE RENT?

LOOK AT THE PICTURE. LOOK AT THE APARTMENT. _____ AT THE MAN. LOOK AT THE WOMAN.

_____ MUCH IS THE APARTMENT? I DON'T KNOW.

_____ IT EXPENSIVE? I DON'T KNOW. IS IT CHEAP?

I _____ KNOW. IS THE APARTMENT BIG? SO-SO.

IS _____ CLEAN? YES.

DO YOU RENT? DO YOU _____ A HOUSE? DO YOU RENT AN APARTMENT? _____ YOUR RENT CHEAP?

I _____

_____

LISTEN AND WRITE

1: _____ A. _____

2: _____ B. _____

1: _____ C. _____

2: _____ D. _____

WRITE A NOTE

(DATE) _____

_____

_____

_____

_____

_____

_____

_____

(SIGNATURE) _____

DIRECTIONS:

PAY THE RENT. WRITE A CHECK.

    RENT: $550—FIVE HUNDRED FIFTY

    LANDLADY: PEGGY DOHERTY

_____ 19 _____

PAY TO THE
ORDER OF _____ $ [_____]

_____ DOLLARS

            _____

LESSON 31 A Trip

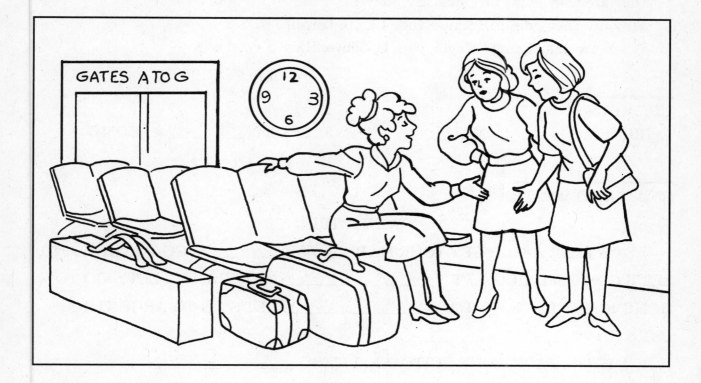

READ ALOUD

1: LOOK AT THE PICTURE.

2: OK.

1: LOOK AT THE SUITCASES.

2: OK.

1: THEY'RE GOING ON A TRIP.

2: RIGHT.

1: LET'S GO, TOO.

2: OK.

DIRECTIONS: LOOK AT THE PICTURE. DRAW. COLOR. WRITE.

1. The big suitcase is brown.
2. The small suitcase is orange.
3. The long suitcase is blue.
4. The woman on the right has red hair.
5. The woman on the left has black hair.
6. The woman in the middle has blonde hair.
7. Look at the clock. It is 11:15.

READ

A TRIP

Look at the picture. Look at the people. Look at the suitcases. They are going on a trip.

Where are they going? To Canada? To Mexico?

How are they going? By bus? By plane?

Why are they going? Because they like to travel?

When are they going? Maybe now. Goodbye. Have a good trip.

UP/DOWN

1. BIG _ _ _ _ _   2. MAN _ _ _ _ _   3. SHORT _ _ _ _   4. COME _ _

READ AND WRITE

TAKE A TRIP

LET'S TAKE A TRIP. GET YOUR MAP. _____ GO TO THAILAND.

LET'S GO TO MEXICO. LET'S _____ TO FRANCE. LET'S GO TO

HONG KONG. LET'S GO TO _____. LET'S GO TO ARGENTINA.

LET'S GO TO _____.

COME ON. PACK YOUR SUITCASE. LET'S _____.

LISTEN AND WRITE

1: _____   A. _____

2: _____   B. _____

1: _____   C. _____

2: _____   D. _____

WRITE A NOTE

(DATE) _____

_____

_____

_____

_____

_____

_____

_____

(SIGNATURE) _____

DIRECTIONS:

LOOK AT THE MAP.

1. Draw a solid yellow line from Vancouver to San Francisco to Mexico City.
2. Draw a dotted red line from New York to Toronto to St. Paul to Seattle.
3. Draw a wavy blue line from Washington, D.C. to Chicago to New Orleans to Managua.
4. Draw a jagged green line from Miami to Houston to Acapulco to San Salvador.

LESSON 32   Take My Picture

FILL OUT

_____
(FAMILY NAME)   (FIRST NAME)   (MIDDLE NAME)

BIRTHDATE _____

READ ALOUD

1: HEY.

2: WHAT?

1: A CAMERA.

2: RIGHT.

1: TAKE MY PICTURE.

2: OK. LOOK AT ME.

1: OK.

2: SMILE.

1: OK.

2: DON'T MOVE.

1: OK.

2: 1–2–3 (CLICK) OK.

DIRECTIONS: LOOK AT THE PICTURE. COLOR. DRAW.

1. The man has a green shirt.

2. The man has black pants.

3. The woman has a blue blouse.

4. The woman has red pants.

5. The woman is holding a large fish in her hands.

6. Look behind the two people. It is a lake. The lake is blue.

7. Draw a small boat in the lake.

8. The camera is black.

READ

A PHOTO

Do you have a camera? Do you have film? Do you like to take pictures? Do you take pictures every day? Do you take pictures every week? Do you take pictures every month?

I have a camera. I have film. I want to take your picture. Look at me. Smile. Don't move. OK.

UP/DOWN

1. FROWN _ _ _ _ _ 2. YOUR _ _ 3. WRONG _ _ _ _ _ 4. NIGHT _ _ _

READ AND WRITE

TAKE MY PICTURE

HEY, YOU HAVE A CAMERA. YOU _____ FILM. TAKE MY PICTURE. I WILL LOOK AT YOU. _____ WILL SMILE. I WON'T MOVE.

I LIKE _____ . I LIKE PICTURES OF ME. I LIKE PICTURES _____ YOU. I LIKE PICTURES OF SCHOOL. I _____ PICTURES OF THIS CITY.

HEY, COME ON. _____ MY PICTURE.

LISTEN AND WRITE

1: _____ A. _____

2: _____ B. _____

1: _____ C. _____

2: _____ D. _____

WRITE A NOTE

(DATE) _____

_____

_____

_____

_____

_____

_____

(SIGNATURE) _____

DIRECTIONS:

Order these reprints:

1. You want **5 inch** reprints.
2. You want **2** reprints of number **1a**.
3. You want **1** reprint of number **2**.
4. You want **4** reprints of number **5a**.
5. You want **3** reprints of number **7a**.
6. You want **6** reprints of number **8**.
7. You want **2** reprints of number **9a**.

ORDER FORM REPRINTS		CHOOSE REPRINT SIZE	☐ 3 INCHES ☐ 5 INCHES			

No.	Quantity	No.	Quantity	No.	Quantity
1		4		7	
1a	*2*	4a		7a	
2		5		8	
2a		5a		8a	
3		6		9	
3a		6a		9a	

LESSON 33 Fire

READ ALOUD

1: HEY, LOOK.

2: A FIRE.

1: RIGHT.

2: EMERGENCY. DIAL 911.

1: NOW?

2: YES, YES. RIGHT NOW.

1: OK, OK.

DIRECTIONS: LOOK AT THE PICTURE.

1. The child has a red dress.
2. The fire fighter has a red hat.
3. The fire fighter has a black coat.
4. Look at the top right window. The fire is orange.
5. Look at the bottom left window. The fire is red.
6. Look at the top left window. The fire is yellow.
7. Look at the bottom right window. The smoke is black.
8. The ladder is brown.

READ

AN EMERGENCY

Look at the picture. Look at the fire. Look at the smoke. Look at the ladder. Look at the fire fighter. Look at the child.

It is an emergency. Dial 911 in an emergency. A fire is an emergency. Dial 911. A robbery is an emergency. Dial 911. An accident is an emergency. Dial 911.

UP/DOWN

1. ADULT __ __ __ __   2. LEFT __ __ __ __   3. TOP __ __ __ · __ __

READ AND WRITE

FIRE

ARE WE HAVING A FIRE? ARE _____ HAVING A FIRE IN SCHOOL? ARE WE HAVING A _____ IN SCHOOL NOW?

LOOK. LOOK OUT _____ DOOR. LOOK DOWNSTAIRS. LOOK UPSTAIRS. LOOK _____ THE NEXT ROOM.

DO YOU SEE A _____? NO? GOOD.

LISTEN AND WRITE

1: _____   A. _____

2: _____   B. _____

1: _____   C. _____

2: _____   D. _____

WRITE A NOTE

(DATE) _____

_____

_____

_____

_____

_____

_____

_____

(SIGNATURE) _____

DIRECTIONS:

MAKE A SIGN.

WRITE:

IN CASE OF FIRE USE STAIRWAY

WRITE:

FIRE HOSE

DIRECTIONS:

Look at the message form.

To: _____ Bob _____

While you were out

DATE _4-27-91_   TIME _4:30_

NAME _Your Wife_

TELEPHONE _417-6000_

☑ called   ☐ will call again
☐ returned your call   ☑ would like you to call
☐ stopped by

MESSAGE: _Call Home, You had a_
small fire in your kitchen.
_____

Person taking message _____ Lee _____

Make out a message form. *Mary called Kim at 2:00, October 17th. Mary's number is 885-5212. Mary will call again. Mary said, "I can't go to school tomorrow." You took the message.*

To: _____

While you were out

DATE _____   TIME _____

NAME _____

TELEPHONE _____

☐ called   ☐ will call again
☐ returned your call   ☐ would like you to call
☐ stopped by

MESSAGE: _____
_____
_____

Person taking message _____

LESSON 34 Radios

READ ALOUD

1: LOOK AT THE PICTURE.
2: OK.
1: THAT'S NOT TV.
2: NO?

1: NO. THAT'S A RADIO.
2: OH.
1: LISTEN TO YOUR RADIO.
2: I LIKE TV.

DIRECTIONS: LOOK AT THE PICTURE. DRAW. COLOR.

1. The man has green pants.
2. The lamp is yellow.
3. The man has glasses.
4. Draw a clock on the wall. It is 7:45.
5. The man has a red sweater.
6. The chair is brown.
7. The vase is blue.
8. The flowers are yellow.
9. Draw a window on the right.
10. Draw the moon outside the window.

READ

LISTEN

Listen. Listen to your radio. Listen to your radio every day.

People listen to radios at home. People listen to radios in their cars. People listen to radios at the beach. People listen to radios on the street.

My radio is small, but I like it. I listen in the morning. I listen in the afternoon. I listen at night. I listen, and listen, and listen.

UP/DOWN

1. TALK _ _ _ _ _   2. BIG _ _ _ _   3. MY _ _ _ _   4. HATE _ _ _ _

READ AND WRITE

MY RADIO

MANY PEOPLE HAVE A RADIO. SOME _____ LISTEN TO MUSIC. SOME PEOPLE LISTEN _____ NEWS. SOME PEOPLE LISTEN TO TALK.

SOME _____ DON'T LIKE TV. THEY LISTEN TO THEIR _____. THEY LISTEN TO THEIR RADIO _____ DAY.

DO YOU HAVE A _____ ?

I _____

_____

LISTEN AND WRITE

1: _____   A. _____

2: _____   B. _____

1: _____   C. _____

2: _____   D. _____

WRITE A NOTE

(DATE) _____

_____

_____

_____

_____

_____

_____

_____

(SIGNATURE) _____

DIRECTIONS:

WRITE THE PROGRAM AT THE RIGHT TIME.

RADIO LOG

Station	FM	6:00	6:30	7:00	7:30
KKHI	101	NEWS	CLASSICS	____	CLASSICS
WFOG	98.6	J. BELL	NEWS	JAZZ	_____
KQED	54.7	____	_____	____	WEATHER
WJAZ	96.3	____	JAZZ	____	JAZZ

1. KQED has **NEWS** at 7:00.
2. WJAZ has **TATUM** at 6:00.
3. KKHI has **WEATHER** at 7:00.
4. WFOG has **MUSIC** at 7:30.
5. KQED has **ROCK 'N ROLL** at 6:00.
6. KQED has **FORUM** at 6:30.
7. WJAZ has **TOP TEN** at 7:00.

LESSON 35   Eat Out

READ ALOUD

1: LOOK AT THE PICTURE.

2: OK.

1: IS HE TIRED?

2: NO.

1: IS HE SICK?

2: NO.

1: WHAT'S THE MATTER?

2: HE'S HUNGRY.

1: I SEE.

DIRECTIONS: LOOK AT THE PICTURE. DRAW. COLOR. WRITE.

1. The man has a blue jacket.

2. Write **RESTAURANT** on the awning.

3. The awning is red, blue, and orange.

4. Look at the sign on the door. Write **OPEN 10:00 A.M. – 9:00 P.M.**

5. The door is yellow.

6. It is night. Draw a moon in the sky.

READ

EAT OUT

Are you hungry? Yes? Eat out. Eat at a restaurant near you.

If you like Chinese food, eat at a Chinese restaurant. If you like Mexican food, eat at a Mexican restaurant. If you like Middle East food, eat at a Middle East restaurant. If you like American food, eat at an American restaurant.

Can I go with you?

UP/DOWN

1. WOMAN _ _ _   2. HEALTHY _ _ _ _   3. FULL _ _ _ _ _ _

READ AND WRITE

A MENU

RESTAURANTS HAVE MENUS. A MENU TELLS YOU _____ NAME OF THE FOOD. A MENU TELLS _____ THE PRICE OF THE FOOD.

ASK FOR _____ MENU IN A RESTAURANT. LOOK AT ALL _____ FOOD. LOOK AT THE PRICES. IF YOU _____ UNDERSTAND, ASK THE WAITER OR THE WAITRESS. THEY _____ HELP YOU.

LISTEN AND WRITE

1: _____   A. _____

2: _____   B. _____

1: _____   C. _____

2: _____   D. _____

DIRECTIONS:

LOOK AT THE MENU.

1. HOW MUCH IS SUSHI? _____

2. HOW MUCH IS COFFEE? _____

3. HOW MUCH IS A TACO? _____

4. HOW MUCH IS A SALAD? _____

5. HOW MUCH IS HA KAW? _____

6. HOW MUCH IS A HAMBURGER? _____

LEE'S RESTAURANT MENU	
HAMBURGER . .	$1.50
TACO	.95
SUSHI	2.50
SALAD	1.00
HA KAW	.60
COFFEE	.40

WRITE A NOTE

(DATE) _____

_____

_____

_____

_____

_____

_____

_____

_____

(SIGNATURE) _____

DIRECTIONS:

MAKE A MENU.

1. WRITE THE RESTAURANT'S NAME.

2. WRITE THE FOOD.

3. WRITE THE PRICE OF THE FOOD.

LESSON 36   A Check-Up

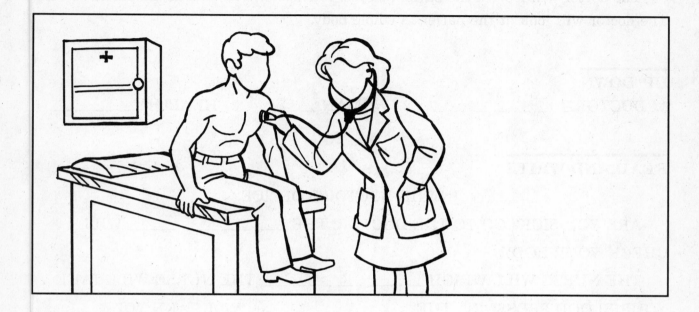

READ ALOUD

1: LOOK AT THE PICTURE.

2: OK.

1: THE PATIENT IS SICK.

2: MAYBE.

1: THE DOCTOR IS LOOKING AT HIM.

2: RIGHT.

1: HE'S HAVING A CHECK-UP.

2: RIGHT.

1: GOOD LUCK.

2: RIGHT.

DIRECTIONS: LOOK AT THE PICTURE. DRAW. COLOR. WRITE.

1. The patient has black pants.

2. Draw the doctor's eyes, nose, and mouth.

3. Draw the patient's eyes, nose, and mouth.

4. Draw a clock on the wall. It is 10:25.

5. The patient has brown shoes.

6. Draw a window in the room.

7. Draw the sun out the window. The sun is yellow.

8. Draw a medicine bottle in the cabinet.

READ

SICK

Look at the picture. Look at the patient. Look at the doctor.

The patient is having a check-up. The doctor is listening to the man's heart.

The doctor will look at the patient's eyes. The doctor will look at the patient's ears. The doctor will look at the patient's whole body.

UP/DOWN

1. DOCTOR _ _ _ _ _ _   2. WOMAN _ _ _   3. HEALTHY _ _ _ _

READ AND WRITE

IN THE DOCTOR'S OFFICE

ARE YOU SICK? GO TO THE DOCTOR. THE _____ WILL CHECK YOUR BODY.

THE NURSE WILL WEIGH _____. THE NURSE WILL TAKE YOUR BLOOD PRESSURE. THE _____ WILL TAKE YOUR TEMPERATURE.

THE DOCTOR WILL _____ AT YOUR EYES. THE DOCTOR WILL LOOK _____ YOUR EARS. THE DOCTOR WILL LOOK AT _____ THROAT. THE DOCTOR WILL TAP YOUR KNEE. THE _____ WILL TAP YOUR CHEST.

RELAX. GOOD LUCK.

LISTEN AND WRITE

1: _____ A. _____

2: _____ B. _____

1: _____ C. _____

2: _____ D. _____

WRITE A NOTE

(DATE) _____

_____

_____

_____

_____

_____

_____

_____

(SIGNATURE) _____

DIRECTIONS:

DRAW YOUR BODY.

1. DRAW YOUR RIGHT ARM AND HAND.

2. DRAW YOUR FACE.

3. DRAW YOUR LEFT LEG.

4. DRAW YOUR LEFT FOOT.

   〉〉〉 = HURTS/ACHES/SORE

5. YOUR LEFT ELBOW HURTS.

6. YOUR HEAD ACHES.

7. YOUR THROAT IS SORE.

8. YOUR LEFT EAR ACHES.

9. YOUR CHEST HURTS.

10. YOUR STOMACH ACHES.

11. YOUR RIGHT HAND HURTS.

12. YOUR LEFT ANKLE HURTS.

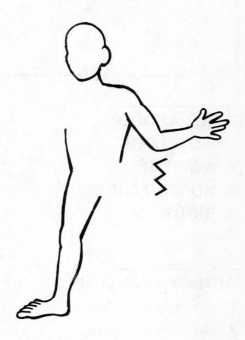

LESSON 37 Mice

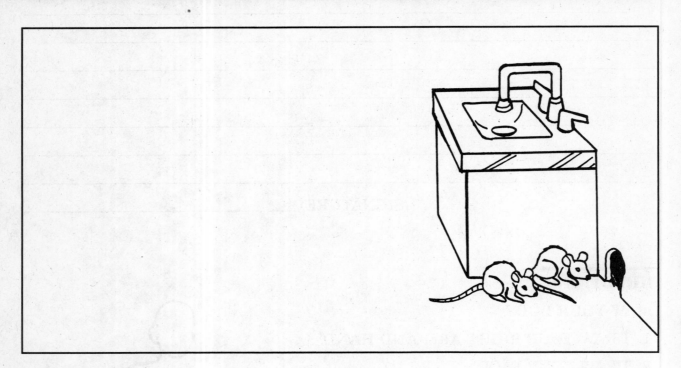

READ ALOUD

1: WOW. LOOK.

2: A MOUSE.

1: NO. TWO MICE.

2: RIGHT.

1: I'M SCARED.

2: RELAX.

1: WRITE THE MANAGER.

2: OK.

DIRECTIONS: LOOK AT THE PICTURE. DRAW. COLOR.

1. One mouse is black.

2. One mouse is gray.

3. Draw a clock on the wall. The time is 1:30.

4. Draw a window in the kitchen.

5. Draw the moon outside the window.

6. Draw a refrigerator in the kitchen.

7. Draw a stove in the kitchen.

READ

MICE

Mice are bad. Do you have mice? Do you have mice in your apartment? Are they in your kitchen? Are they in your bedroom? Are they in your living room? Are you scared? Yes?

Tell your manager. Write your manager. Call your manager. Complain to your manager. Now.

UP/DOWN

1. GOOD __ __ __   2. OUT __ __   3. MY __ __ __ __   4. NO __ __ __

READ AND WRITE

A MOUSE

I HAVE A MOUSE IN MY APARTMENT. _____ HAVE A SMALL GRAY MOUSE IN _____ KITCHEN. I HATE IT.

MICE ARE DIRTY. _____ EAT FOOD. MICE SCARE PEOPLE.

I AM _____ TO TELL MY MANAGER. I AM GOING _____ CALL MY MANAGER. I AM GOING TO WRITE MY _____ NOW.

LISTEN AND WRITE

1: _____   A. _____

2: _____   B. _____

1: _____   C. _____

2: _____   D. _____

WRITE A NOTE

(DATE) _____

_____

_____

_____

_____

_____

_____

_____

(SIGNATURE) _____

DIRECTIONS:

WRITE YOUR MANAGER. TELL HIM YOUR NAME AND APARTMENT. YOU HAVE
MICE. THEY EAT YOUR FOOD. THEY CHEW YOUR SHOES. THEY ARE DIRTY.
THEY SCARE YOUR CHILDREN. YOU HATE MICE. YOU NEED A MOUSE TRAP.
YOU NEED POISON.

_____

_____

_____

_____

_____

_____

_____

_____

LESSON 38 A Job

READ ALOUD

1: I WANT A JOB.

2: LOOK FOR ONE.

1: WHERE?

2: LOOK IN THE NEWSPAPER.

1: OK.

2: ASK YOUR FRIENDS.

1: OK.

2: GO TO AN EMPLOYMENT OFFICE.

1: OK. THANKS.

DIRECTIONS: LOOK AT THE PICTURE. DRAW. COLOR. WRITE.

1. The man has a brown suit.

2. The woman has a blue dress.

3. Draw a phone on the desk.

4. Draw a clock on the wall. The time is 3:40.

5. Write **U.S. EMPLOYMENT AGENCY** on the wall.

6. The man is holding a newspaper.

READ

A JOB INTERVIEW

Look at the picture. The man is at a job interview. He is looking for a job. The interviewer is interviewing the man. She is talking to him. She is asking him questions.

Will he get a job? Maybe.

UP/DOWN

1. HE __ __ __   2. TELL __ __ __   3. MY __ __ __ __   4. COME __ __

READ AND WRITE

AT AN INTERVIEW

JOB INTERVIEWERS ASK QUESTIONS. THEY ASK, "WHAT

_____ YOUR NAME?" THEY ASK, "WHAT IS YOUR

_____ ?" THEY ASK, "WHAT IS YOUR TELEPHONE NUMBER?"

_____ ASK, "WHAT CAN YOU DO?" THEY ASK,

"_____ YOU SPEAK ENGLISH?"

THEY SOMETIMES ASK, "HOW _____ MONEY DO YOU WANT?"

LISTEN AND WRITE

1: _____   A. _____

2: _____   B. _____

1: _____   C. _____

2: _____   D. _____

WRITE A NOTE

(DATE) _____

_____

_____

_____

_____

_____

_____

_____

(SIGNATURE) _____

DIRECTIONS:

LOOK AT THE EMPLOYMENT ADS.

A. COOK, English spking, live-in, benefits. 861−8187.

B. COUPLE, Live-in, 6 days per wk. Non smk. Must be a good cook, hskpr, gardner, love kids, speak English. 885−5212.

C. MOTEL, Mgrs motel, Exp'd couple. Exc salary + roomy apt. 848−2244.

D. APPLIANCE & Refrig Repair Person, Transp & Equip nec. 621−7512.

E. BAKER, Baker/mixer, reliable, self-starter. 552−0161.

WHICH TELEPHONE NUMBER WILL YOU CALL?

1. ____−_____ I'm a good cook. I hate to do housework.

2. ____−_____ I bake wonderful bread.

3. ____−_____ I owned a small hotel in my country.

4. ____−_____ I can repair anything.

5. ____−_____ My wife and I are good cooks and we keep our house clean.

LESSON 39   A Garage Sale

READ ALOUD

1: LOOK AT THE PICTURE.

2: WOW. A GARAGE SALE.

1: RIGHT.

2: EVERYTHING IS CHEAP.

1: RIGHT.

2: BARGAIN.

1: RIGHT.

2: LET'S GO.

1: OK.

DIRECTIONS: LOOK AT THE PICTURE. COLOR.DRAW. WRITE.

1. The woman has a red dress.
2. The woman has a yellow hat.
3. The small chair is blue.
4. The clock is orange.
5. The TV is brown.
6. She is holding a green jacket.
7. The flowers are pink. The vase is purple.
8. Write SALE on the sign on the chair.
9. Draw the sun in the sky. It is yellow.

READ

GARAGE SALES

Garage sales are useful. People sell used things. People sell used chairs. People sell used clothes. People sell used pots and pans. People sell used dishes. People sell used TVs. People sell used radios. People sell used clocks.

Everything is cheap, but bargain. Come on. Let's go to a garage sale.

UP/DOWN

1. BUY _ _ _ _ 2. EXPENSIVE _ _ _ _ _ 3. GO _ _ _ _ 4. NEW _ _ _ _

READ AND WRITE

BARGAIN

I LIKE GARAGE SALES. I LIKE _____ BARGAIN. IF I SEE A

COAT, AND _____ LIKE IT, AND I WANT IT, I _____.

I SAY, "HOW MUCH?"

THEY SAY, "$5.00."

_____ SAY, "THAT'S TOO MUCH. I WILL _____

YOU $2.50." THEY SAY, "NO. $4.00."

I _____, "THAT IS TOO MUCH. I WILL GIVE _____

$3.00." THEY SAY, "NO. $3.50."

I SAY, "I WILL _____ YOU $3.25."

THEY SAY, "OK $3.25."

I _____, "OK. THANKS."

LISTEN AND WRITE

1: _____ A. _____

2: _____ B. _____

1: _____ C. _____

2: _____ D. _____

WRITE A NOTE

(DATE) _____

_____

_____

_____

_____

_____

_____

_____

(SIGNATURE) _____

DIRECTIONS:

YOU BOUGHT A COAT AT A GARAGE SALE. THE COAT WAS $3.25 (THREE AND 25/100). THE SELLER WAS PAUL NIXON. WRITE A CHECK.

_____ 19 _____

PAY TO THE
ORDER OF _____ $ [_____]

_____ DOLLARS

LESSON 40 Payday

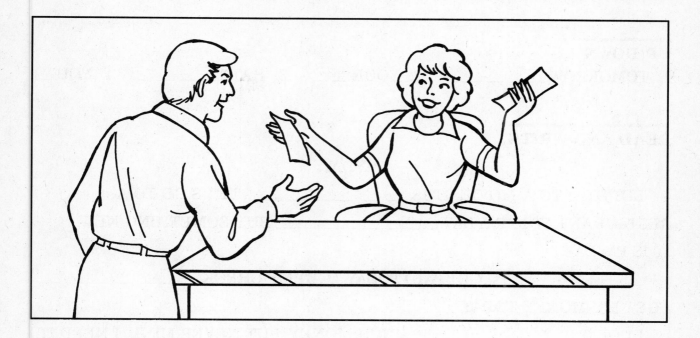

READ ALOUD

1: HEY.

2: WHAT?

1: IT'S PAYDAY.

2: TODAY?

1: RIGHT.

2: WOW. GOOD. I'M BROKE.

DIRECTIONS: LOOK AT THE PICTURE. DRAW. COLOR. WRITE.

1. The woman behind the desk has a red blouse.
2. The man has a blue shirt and brown pants.
3. Draw a clock on the wall. It is 3:00.
4. Draw a calendar on the wall.
5. Draw a company sign on the wall. It says **WOLF COMPANY.**
6. Draw a telephone on the desk.
7. Draw a vase with flowers on the desk.

READ

PAYDAY

Today is payday. I like payday. I can pay my bills.

I can pay my telephone bill. I can pay my water bill. I can pay my gas and electric bill. I can pay my rent. I can pay my car payment.

Hey, I can go to a movie. I'm not broke now. Wow.

UP/DOWN

1. TOMORROW _ _ _ _   2. YOUR _ _   3. HATE _ _ _ _   4. YOU _

READ AND WRITE

PAYDAY

LET'S GO TO A MOVIE. IT IS _____. LET'S GO TO A RESTAURANT. IT IS PAYDAY. _____ BUY SOMETHING NEW. IT IS PAYDAY.

_____ GET PAID TODAY. I GET MY CHECK _____. I GET MY MONEY TODAY.

I DON'T _____ MUCH MONEY, BUT NEVER MIND, I NEED IT. I _____ BROKE.

LISTEN AND WRITE

1: _____   A. _____

2: _____   B. _____

1: _____   C. _____

2: _____   D. _____

WRITE A NOTE

(DATE) _____

_____

_____

_____

_____

_____

_____

_____

(SIGNATURE) _____

MY PAYSTUB

EARNINGS	HOURS	AMOUNT	DEDUCTIONS		PAYROLL PERIOD
REGULAR		$725.00	FICA TAX	59.28	06-06-91 TO 06-21-91
			STATE TX	8.43	
			UNION	8.03	
			FED TAX	127.55	
			SDI	9.47	
GROSS EARNINGS		$725.00	TOTAL DEDUC	$212.76	NET PAY $511.24

DIRECTIONS:

LOOK AT THE PAYSTUB. ANSWER THE QUESTIONS.

1. HOW MUCH MONEY CAN I TAKE HOME? _____

2. HOW MUCH IS MY STATE TAX? _____

3. HOW MUCH IS MY FEDERAL TAX? _____

4. HOW MUCH IS MY UNION DUES? _____

5. HOW MUCH IS MY SOCIAL SECURITY? _____

6. HOW MUCH IS MY TOTAL EARNINGS? _____

MAKE YOUR PAYSTUB:

EARNINGS	HOURS	AMOUNT	DEDUCTIONS		PAYROLL PERIOD
	_____	$_____	FICA TAX	$_____	_____
			STATE TX	_____	
			UNION	_____	
			FED TAX	_____	
			SDI	_____	
GROSS EARNINGS		$_____	TOTAL DEDUC	_____	NET PAY $_____

SUPPLEMENT 1
Special Washington's Birthday

FILL OUT

NAME _____
        (LAST NAME)   (FIRST NAME)   (MIDDLE NAME)

ADDRESS _____
            (NUMBER)   (STREET)   (APT. #)

_____
(CITY)   (STATE)   (ZIP)

READ ALOUD

1: LOOK AT THE PICTURE.

2: OK.

1: LOOK AT THE FATHER.

2: OK.

1: LOOK AT THE SON.

2: OK.

1: LOOK AT GEORGE WASHINGTON.

2: WOW.

DIRECTIONS: LOOK AT THE PICTURE. DRAW. COLOR.

1. Draw the father's eyes, nose, and mouth.

2. The father has a blue jacket.

3. The son has a red shirt.

4. The father has glasses.

5. The picture frame is yellow.

READ

THE FIRST PRESIDENT

George Washington was President. George Washington was President of the United States. George Washington was the first President of the United States.

Some people said, "Be our king."

George Washington said, "No, thanks. Elect me President."

And the people did.

UP/DOWN

1. FATHER __ __ __   2. FIRST __ __ __ __   3. YOU __   4. SHE __ __

READ AND WRITE

GEORGE WASHINGTON

LOOK AT THE PICTURE. LOOK AT THE FATHER. _____ AT THE SON. LOOK AT GEORGE WASHINGTON.

_____ WASHINGTON WAS THE FIRST PRESIDENT. GEORGE WASHINGTON _____ THE FIRST PRESIDENT OF THE UNITED STATES. GEORGE _____ WAS THE FIRST PRESIDENT OF THE UNITED _____ OF AMERICA.

GEORGE WASHINGTON WAS THE FATHER OF THE U.S.A.

I _____

_____

LISTEN AND WRITE

1: _____ A. _____

2: _____ B. _____

1: _____ C. _____

2: _____ D. _____

WRITE A NOTE

(DATE) _____

_____

  _____

_____

_____

_____

_____

_____

_____

(SIGNATURE) _____

DIRECTIONS:

MAKE A U.S. ONE DOLLAR BILL.

SUPPLEMENT 2 Christmas

READ ALOUD

1: LOOK AT THE PICTURE.

2: WOW.

1: A CHRISTMAS TREE.

2: WOW.

1: DECORATED.

2: WOW.

1: MERRY CHRISTMAS.

2: SAME TO YOU.

DIRECTIONS: LOOK AT THE PICTURE. DRAW. COLOR.

1. The Christmas tree is green.

2. The Christmas lights are red, and blue, and orange.

3. The Christmas decorations are red, and purple, and yellow.

4. The Christmas tree has a star on top. It is yellow. Draw it.

5. Draw Christmas presents under the tree.

6. Draw a clock on the wall. It is 5:45.

7. Draw a big window behind the tree.

8. Draw the moon out the window.

READ

CHRISTMAS

Christmas is a holiday. Christmas is a holiday in many countries. Christmas is a holiday in North America. Christmas is a holiday in South America. Christmas is a holiday in New Zealand. Christmas is a holiday in Europe. Christmas is a holiday in Australia. Christmas is a holiday in Central America.

Is Christmas a holiday where you come from?

UP/DOWN

1. WORK DAY _ _ _ _ _ _ _ 2. LAST _ _ _ _ _ _ 3. I _ _ _ 4. ME _ _ _

READ AND WRITE

CHRISTMAS

MANY PEOPLE LIKE CHRISTMAS. WOMEN LIKE CHRISTMAS.

_____ LIKE CHRISTMAS. OLD PEOPLE LIKE CHRISTMAS. YOUNG

_____ LIKE CHRISTMAS. CHILDREN LIKE CHRISTMAS THE MOST.

_____ PEOPLE HAVE A CHRISTMAS TREE. THEY PUT LIGHTS

_____ THE TREE. THEY PUT DECORATIONS ON THE

_____ . THEY PUT TINSEL ON THE TREE. THEY _____

POPCORN ON THE TREE. THEY PUT A _____ ON THE TREE TOP.

A CHRISTMAS TREE _____ A BEAUTIFUL THING.

I _____

_____

LISTEN AND WRITE

1: _____   A. _____

2: _____   B. _____

1: _____   C. _____

2: _____   D. _____

WRITE A NOTE

(DATE) _____

_____

_____

_____

_____

_____

_____

_____

_____

(SIGNATURE) _____

DIRECTIONS:
DRAW A CHRISTMAS TREE.

APPENDIXES

19

19

19

STUDENT DICTIONARY

A

_____ _____ _____ _____
_____ _____ _____ _____
_____ _____ _____ _____
_____ _____ _____ _____
_____ _____ _____ _____
_____ _____ _____ _____
_____ _____ _____ _____
_____ _____ _____ _____
_____ _____ _____ _____
_____ _____ _____ _____
_____ _____ _____ _____
_____ _____ _____ _____
_____ _____ _____ _____

B

_____   _____   _____   _____
_____   _____   _____   _____
_____   _____   _____   _____
_____   _____   _____   _____
_____   _____   _____   _____
_____   _____   _____   _____
_____   _____   _____   _____
_____   _____   _____   _____
_____   _____   _____   _____
_____   _____   _____   _____
_____   _____   _____   _____
_____   _____   _____   _____
_____   _____   _____   _____
_____   _____   _____   _____

C

_____   _____   _____   _____

_____   _____   _____   _____

_____   _____   _____   _____

_____   _____   _____   _____

_____   _____   _____   _____

_____   _____   _____   _____

_____   _____   _____   _____

_____   _____   _____   _____

_____   _____   _____   _____

_____   _____   _____   _____

_____   _____   _____   _____

_____   _____   _____   _____

_____   _____   _____   _____

_____   _____   _____   _____

_____   _____   _____   _____

_____   _____   _____   _____

_____   _____   _____   _____

_____   _____   _____   _____

D

_____   _____   _____   _____
_____   _____   _____   _____
_____   _____   _____   _____
_____   _____   _____   _____
_____   _____   _____   _____
_____   _____   _____   _____
_____   _____   _____   _____
_____   _____   _____   _____
_____   _____   _____   _____
_____   _____   _____   _____

E

_____   _____   _____   _____
_____   _____   _____   _____
_____   _____   _____   _____
_____   _____   _____   _____
_____   _____   _____   _____
_____   _____   _____   _____
_____   _____   _____   _____
_____   _____   _____   _____
_____   _____   _____   _____
_____   _____   _____   _____

F

G

H

_____   _____   _____   _____

_____   _____   _____   _____

_____   _____   _____   _____

_____   _____   _____   _____

_____   _____   _____   _____

_____   _____   _____   _____

_____   _____   _____   _____

_____   _____   _____   _____

_____   _____   _____   _____

_____   _____   _____   _____

I

_____   _____   _____   _____

_____   _____   _____   _____

_____   _____   _____   _____

_____   _____   _____   _____

_____   _____   _____   _____

_____   _____   _____   _____

_____   _____   _____   _____

_____   _____   _____   _____

_____   _____   _____   _____

_____   _____   _____   _____

J

_____   _____   _____   _____

_____   _____   _____   _____

_____   _____   _____   _____

_____   _____   _____   _____

_____   _____   _____   _____

_____   _____   _____   _____

_____   _____   _____   _____

K

_____   _____   _____   _____

_____   _____   _____   _____

_____   _____   _____   _____

_____   _____   _____   _____

_____   _____   _____   _____

_____   _____   _____   _____

_____   _____   _____   _____

L

_____ _____ _____ _____

_____ _____ _____ _____

_____ _____ _____ _____

_____ _____ _____ _____

_____ _____ _____ _____

_____ _____ _____ _____

_____ _____ _____ _____

_____ _____ _____ _____

_____ _____ _____ _____

M

_____ _____ _____ _____

_____ _____ _____ _____

_____ _____ _____ _____

_____ _____ _____ _____

_____ _____ _____ _____

_____ _____ _____ _____

_____ _____ _____ _____

_____ _____ _____ _____

_____ _____ _____ _____

_____ _____ _____ _____

_____ _____ _____ _____

_____ _____ _____ _____

_____ _____ _____ _____

_____ _____ _____ _____

N

O

P

_____   _____   _____   _____

_____   _____   _____   _____

_____   _____   _____   _____

_____   _____   _____   _____

_____   _____   _____   _____

_____   _____   _____   _____

_____   _____   _____   _____

_____   _____   _____   _____

_____   _____   _____   _____

_____   _____   _____   _____

_____   _____   _____   _____

_____   _____   _____   _____

_____   _____   _____   _____

Q

_____   _____   _____   _____

_____   _____   _____   _____

_____   _____   _____   _____

_____   _____   _____   _____

_____   _____   _____   _____

_____   _____   _____   _____

R

S

_____   _____   _____   _____
_____   _____   _____   _____
_____   _____   _____   _____
_____   _____   _____   _____
_____   _____   _____   _____
_____   _____   _____   _____
_____   _____   _____   _____
_____   _____   _____   _____
_____   _____   _____   _____
_____   _____   _____   _____
_____   _____   _____   _____
_____   _____   _____   _____
_____   _____   _____   _____
_____   _____   _____   _____
_____   _____   _____   _____
_____   _____   _____   _____
_____   _____   _____   _____
_____   _____   _____   _____

T

_____ _____ _____ _____
_____ _____ _____ _____
_____ _____ _____ _____
_____ _____ _____ _____
_____ _____ _____ _____
_____ _____ _____ _____
_____ _____ _____ _____
_____ _____ _____ _____
_____ _____ _____ _____
_____ _____ _____ _____
_____ _____ _____ _____
_____ _____ _____ _____
_____ _____ _____ _____

U

_____ _____ _____ _____
_____ _____ _____ _____
_____ _____ _____ _____
_____ _____ _____ _____
_____ _____ _____ _____
_____ _____ _____ _____
_____ _____ _____ _____

V

_____	_____	_____	_____
_____	_____	_____	_____
_____	_____	_____	_____
_____	_____	_____	_____
_____	_____	_____	_____
_____	_____	_____	_____
_____	_____	_____	_____

W

_____	_____	_____	_____
_____	_____	_____	_____
_____	_____	_____	_____
_____	_____	_____	_____
_____	_____	_____	_____
_____	_____	_____	_____
_____	_____	_____	_____
_____	_____	_____	_____
_____	_____	_____	_____
_____	_____	_____	_____
_____	_____	_____	_____
_____	_____	_____	_____
_____	_____	_____	_____
_____	_____	_____	_____
_____	_____	_____	_____

X

_____   _____   _____   _____
_____   _____   _____   _____
_____   _____   _____   _____
_____   _____   _____   _____
_____   _____   _____   _____
_____   _____   _____   _____
_____   _____   _____   _____
_____   _____   _____   _____
_____   _____   _____   _____
_____   _____   _____   _____

Y

_____   _____   _____   _____
_____   _____   _____   _____
_____   _____   _____   _____
_____   _____   _____   _____
_____   _____   _____   _____
_____   _____   _____   _____
_____   _____   _____   _____
_____   _____   _____   _____
_____   _____   _____   _____
_____   _____   _____   _____

Z

_____ _____ _____ _____
_____ _____ _____ _____
_____ _____ _____ _____
_____ _____ _____ _____
_____ _____ _____ _____
_____ _____ _____ _____
_____ _____ _____ _____
_____ _____ _____ _____
_____ _____ _____ _____
_____ _____ _____ _____
_____ _____ _____ _____